The Arrow Valley, Herefordshire: Archaeology, Landscape Change and Conservation

Paul White

With a contribution by
Mark Macklin and colleagues
University of Wales, Aberystwyth

2003

Published by
Herefordshire Archaeology
Herefordshire Council
PO Box 144
Hereford
HR1 2YN
(*Phone:* 01432 383351; *Fax:* 01432 383354)

Printed by
Orphans Press Ltd.
Laundry Lane
Hereford Road
Leominster
Herefordshire
HR6 8JT

ISBN: 0-9546998-0-7

HSA Series Editor
Keith Ray
Layout and formatting
PA White

Front cover: The line of Rowe Ditch spanning the landscape of the Arrow Valley. ©HAAS 03-CN-0601

The Arrow Valley project was funded as a partnership study, with contributions from English Heritage, Herefordshire Council and the Herefordshire Rivers LEADER+ project (European Union and DEFRA).

Herefordshire Studies in Archaeology is the monograph publication series of Herefordshire Archaeology. In addition the county archaeological service produces a report series, Herefordshire Archaeology Reports

Contents

List of Illustrations

Figures

List of Tables

Table

Abbreviations

CPAT- Clwyd-Powys Archaeological Trust
HAAS- Herefordshire Archaeology Aerial Survey
HSM- Herefordshire Sites and Monuments
MASH- Millennium Air Survey of Herefordshire
RCHME- Royal Commission on Historic Monuments for England
TWNFC- Transactions of the Woolhope Naturalists' Field Club
WNFC- Woolhope Naturalists' Field Club

Acknowledgements

The Arrow Valley Archaeology, Landscape Change and Conservation project was only possible with the help and co- operation of the community. However without the financial support of The Herefordshire Rivers LEADER+ Local Action Group, English Heritage and Herefordshire Council this project could not have been developed. The support of David Guy, Project Manager for LEADER+ Herefordshire Rivers, and Kathy Perrin, English Heritage Project Officer, is acknowledged here.

The originality of the project and its development from informal discussions to a full investigation of the landscape is due to the County Archaeologist, Dr. Keith Ray. Not only did he comment on many versions of this text but provided a steering hand throughout the project. The excavations, field surveys and maintenance of the fieldwork records would not have been to the high standard achieved without the assistance of Cori Renfrew. Throughout the course of the project other members of Herefordshire Archaeology assisted the project and their help was gratefully received and is acknowledged here; Tim Hoverd, Richard Lello, David Williams, Rebecca Rosseff, Melissa Seddon, Miranda Greene, Toria Forsyth-Moser and Laura Shakespeare.

The excellent work of Professor Mark Macklin and his team in the investigation of the Holocene geomorphology of the landscape is recognised here. Discussion and advice on- site during the excavations from Eric Johnstone was warmly received and provided a new insight into reading the landscape. Advice from Lisa Moffet, English Heritage West Midlands Scientific Advisor, is acknowledged and Judith Leigh, English Heritage Field Monument Warden, is also thanked for her support during the project. Artefact specialists (Alex Gibson, Martyn Barber and C. Jane Evans) are thanked for the fast appraisal and production of their reports that have assisted in our understanding of the investigated sites.

The involvement of the community was paramount for the success of the project and the enthusiasm and tireless promotion of the project by Tony Norman is acknowledged here. Not only did Mr. Norman raise awareness of the project but also volunteered for the first farm survey. The owner of Staunton-on-Arrow motte, Miss. A. Brisbane is heartily thanked for her commitment to the scrub management works upon the monument and thanks to Peter Burton for undertaking and co- ordinating the work along with Tony Norman. Thanks are also given to Mike Williams for his support of the project and his words of encouragement throughout. Numerous landowners and farmers were involved in the project and they are thanked here. Mr. Watkins of Lower Burton, Austin Owens and Tony Norman and family are thanked for permitting the site investigations upon their land at such short notice. Austin and his family are also thanked for taking part in the whole farm survey of their land. Grateful thanks are also due to Colin Andrews, Susan Bowen, Edward Bulmer, Andrew Connop and family, Lindy Connop and Shelly Price, Gerry Corfield, David Forbes, Richard Hall, Ian and William Laurie, Hugh Lowe, David Owens and Clive and Juliet Williams, for their participation in the whole farm surveys. Further thanks are due to David Owens and Colin Andrews for contributing their time and judgement in the selection of the geomorphological contractors involved in this project.

Members of the community took part in the investigations including Gerald Ford, Chris High, Barbara Joss, Michael Moore, Roger Pearce, Geoff Steel, Joan Truckle, Terry White and Paul Wood. The excavations at Admarsh were only possible with the involvement of members of the Eardisland Oral History Group and in particular the involvement of Paul Selfe. The project also provided an opportunity for students to take part and their invaluable contribution is acknowledged here; Tim Duckett, Huw Groucett, Sam Meadows, Ashleigh Taylor, Nick Vaughan and James Chester-Masters. There were many more members of the community that participated in the project through the organised events. Although too numerous to list here, their interest and enthusiasm is appreciated here.

Ink drawings within this report are by Tim Hoverd. Chris Musson took the aerial photographs reproduced here. Each photograph carries its own copyright and reference number. Photography was taken over a numer of years but is recorded as being for the Clwyd-Powys Archaeological Trust, for the field name section of the Woolhope Naturalists' Field Club as part of the Millennium Aerial Survey of Herefordshire and most recently for the Herefordshire Archaeology Aerial Survey.

Foreword

Landscape change is an everyday fact of life, so why study it in detail? The answer from an archaeological perspective is inextricably linked to the question of past present and future survival of remains that are the source materials from which archaeologists write history. The answer is therefore also closely linked to 'conservation'. In common parlance, conservation is about resisting change, but in fact, it concerns rather a process more akin to the stewardship of fish stocks in the oceans, with one important difference. That difference is that in the maintenance of levels of population of fish, replenishment is possible. Remains from the past are both finite – in the sense that we cannot go back in time and recreate archaeological deposits – and are by definition continually being erased by activities associated with inhabiting the same place in the present day, as well as by natural processes of erosion.

Stewardship and conservation are therefore about managing change, erosion and loss, rather than the prevention of these things. In order to manage anything, we have to be as fully aware as possible of its characteristics. To register the impact of change, we must achieve an understanding of the nature of the processes and actions concerned. In this way, studies of archaeology, landscape change and conservation are necessarily linked. In the series of projects being developed by Herefordshire Archaeology as part of the Herefordshire Rivers LEADER+ project, the aim is to add a further dimension to such studies: the involvement of the local community in a variety of ways in different aspects of exploration and conservation.

The present report marks the end of a 'pilot' stage in such work, that has involved the marshalling of established ways of looking at the landscape (landscape history, archaeological site investigations, and geomorphological study of river development), combined with innovative ways of characterising local distinctiveness and historic trends. The project developed out of work by the county archaeological service from 1999, concerned with characterising the historic landscape of the county as a whole, and with looking at the impact of particular processes of erosion, such as arable farming.

Herefordshire's archaeology is both diverse and under- explored. It is rich and varied, but has been particularly vulnerable to the nature of change that has occurred in the farmed landscape over the past thirty years. With arable intensification has come loss of boundaries, permanent pasture and traditional orchards. Within the new arable fields, heavier machinery, new rotational practices, and the advent of particular forms of cash-cropping on contract, has led to a level of erosion of buried remains that is unprecedented in the history of the area. However, in landscape terms, this extent of arable is not new. Archaeological survey work over the past five years has demonstrated convincingly that a yet larger area of the land surface was under cultivation at around AD 1300.

So landscape change is both continual and cyclical. Within this context, river valleys are locations that have experienced quite dramatic episodes of change during the centuries across which they have been occupied by human communities. While we 'know' this fact in reference to other parts of Britain, it is one of the achievements of the present study that we have now begun to document this process closely in at least one of Herefordshire's river valleys.

Dr. Keith Ray
County Archaeologist
Herefordshire Council

PROJECT SUMMARY

Aims, approaches and activities

The Arrow Valley Archaeology, Landscape Change and Conservation Project (AVALCCP) was carried out during 2003. It was organised as a pilot project for a proposed project series within the broader Herefordshire Rivers LEADER+ project. The AVALCCP was a partnership project between Herefordshire Archaeology and the Arrow Valley Farmers group. It sought to further a number of the key aims of the LEADER+ project programme, while more generally advancing knowledge and appreciation of the county's archaeology.

In particular, five of the LEADER+ project aims were specifically addressed via the AVALCCP. These were:

- Priority theme 1.1, to 'explore the history and identity of the area'
- Theme 3.1, to 'raise awareness of the heritage and cultural aspects of the rivers, floodplains and valleys'
- Theme 3.2, to 'engage local people/communities in the process of change'
- Theme 4.1, to 'promote proper management of the river valleys and floodplains', and
- Theme 4.2, 'to monitor the effects of change within river catchments'.

The project addressed these aims through a number of landscape survey initiatives and site-based studies, through conservation works and seminars, and through the provision of information in a variety of ways. This work involved professional archaeologists and geologists, and members of the local community, in direct studies of the landscape that engaged and informed other local residents and landowners.

These studies featured in particular:

- Mapping visits in the landscape, to trace old stream channels (geomorphology), and to assess survival and discovery potential (archaeology).

- Farm visits, to locate key heritage features, assess patterns of past and present land-use and to note former constructed watercourses, channels and other water-related features (archaeology).

- Site based investigations to follow up discoveries, to provide information on sites seen from the air, and to assess processes of erosion and deposition affecting such sites (archaeology and geomorphology).

- Site based conservation works, principally at Staunton-on-Arrow, and the provision of conservation and historical information to farmers, landowners and residents (archaeology, Arrow Farmers).

- A very full programme of talks, guided landscape walks, seminars, farm visits, workshops and other events (such as a finds roadshow).

What this series of activities represented, in turn, was:

- The first ever study of the development of the Arrow Valley river system.

- The first deployment of modern geomorphological survey and dating techniques over a whole river system in Herefordshire.

- The first ever landscape-wide survey of the conservation status of the farmed landscape in the county.

· The first ever linked series of whole farm historic environment studies.

· The first linked series of archaeological field investigations specifically carried out in tandem with geomorphological study in the county.

· The first wide-scale community archaeology partnership project in Herefordshire, directly involving resident members of the local community.

· The first linked provision of information within an immediate and limited time-frame – including production and dissemination of this report.

Results

The project produced a series of 'headline' results:

· Archaeology

The landscape and site-based studies provided the beginnings of a new framework for understanding previous archaeological discoveries. They also created a starting point for appreciating the origins and development of settlement here, particularly in close proximity to the River Arrow in its middle reaches.

These studies included site investigations at Staunton-on-Arrow, that dated the aerially visible enclosures to the Iron Age (800BC to AD50). More significantly still in a national context, they also revealed an unsuspected early multi-phase prehistoric settlement, the latest period of use of which was dated c.2000-1600BC.

The studies also included site investigations at The Leen, Pembridge, that provided a date *after which* the major Herefordshire linear earthwork monument 'Rowe Ditch' (previously undated) was constructed, from AD 200. The same investigations produced evidence for the origins of local field systems in the Iron Age, and for the development of farms here during the Roman period.

· Landscape change

Archaeological and geomorphological studies provided a considerable amount of evidence for the development of the river catchment, and especially for the movement of river channels across the floodplain.

This included comprehensive field mapping of former river channels, especially in the middle and lower reaches of the river. It provided some evidence to date such movements at four locations. Active erosion of new channels and filling of old channels meant that some archaeological monuments from earlier ages were in part swept away, while some deposits were deeply buried.

This is a process that has been going on since the end of the latest Ice Age (c.12,000 years ago), but these new studies are showing particular phases of dramatic activity – for instance around the middle years of the Roman period in Britain – c.AD200.

· **Conservation**

Archaeological studies of the present landscape produced further insights into the nature and pace of landscape change in the twentieth century.

Awareness of issues of archaeological survival, river dynamics and conservation problems for the historic environment was raised significantly during the project.

A major field monument characteristic of the legacy of Norman supremacy in the Marches was cleared of obscuring vegetation. This has 'reinscribed' within the landscape an important feature of the local historic environment near to the River Arrow.

Practical means of enacting historic conservation have been discussed with a varied group of local farmers and landowners.

A whole new generation of local residents has been informed of the presence of landscape features of historic significance, and has realised the potential of focussed, professionally co-ordinated surveys and site investigations.

The landscape-wide survey of standing buildings has contributed towards the practical definition of local distinctiveness.

PART ONE

INTRODUCTION TO THE ARROW VALLEY PROJECT

Chapter 1

The project in the context of the Herefordshire Rivers programme

The Arrow Valley Archaeology, Landscape Change and Conservation project began in February 2003 and continued for the following nine months, concluding at the end of October.

This report is the result of the work undertaken as part of this project, which was supported and funded by The Herefordshire Rivers LEADER+ project, English Heritage and Herefordshire Council. The Arrow Valley is located to the west of Leominster in Northwest Herefordshire (Figure 1). Within the LEADER+ Herefordshire Rivers project area the River Arrow flows through ten modern day parishes (Huntington, Kington Rural, Kington, Lyonshall, Titley, Staunton- on- Arrow, Pembridge, Eardisland, Monkland and Stretford, and Leominster). These parishes have therefore provided the geographical frame for the Arrow Valley Archaeology, Landscape Change and Conservation Project (Figure 2).

The River Arrow rises in the Welsh hills, to the south of Llanfihangel nant Melan. The river is a tributary of the River Lugg and its confluence with that river is approximately 40km to the east (along its course). Around 34km of that course lies within Herefordshire. The confluence is located just to the south of Leominster near Stoke Prior. The Arrow flows eastwards from the Welsh Border through the steep valleys of Huntington and Kington Rural with a narrow river valley through the upland landscape. To the east of Staunton -on- Arrow the valley widens and the sinuosity of the river increases in frequency as it flows through the parishes of Pembridge, Eardisland and Monkland.

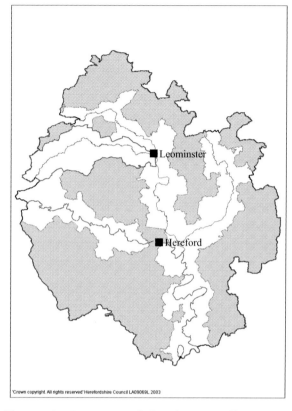

Figure 1 Location of the Arrow Valley within Herefordshire

The overall aims of the Herefordshire Rivers project are to improve conservation measures, to provide environmental interpretation and related events, and to celebrate the heritage through activities that involve the community. The LEADER + project seeks the development of local initiatives organised and sometimes also operated by local community groups, or led by local agencies with community support, in fulfilment of its project aims.

Four key objectives of the LEADER+ Herefordshire Rivers project were defined to seek to identify opportunities to:

·   enhance the distinctiveness of the local countryside (both cultural/ historical features and wildlife/ habitats/ landscapes)

· use local environmental and cultural resources for economic and recreational purposes

· increase environmental knowledge and skills

· revitalise natural processes inherent in the County's river systems.

The construction of a programme of archaeological and conservation based projects was envisaged at the time that the LEADER+ project was devised. It was clear therefore that the work of such a programme could fulfil some aspects of the ambitions expressed in the LEADER+ objectives. Herefordshire Archaeology therefore developed proposals for a programme that would combine archaeological survey, investigation and local management works.

The intention was also to organise a programme of activities that would serve to explain, and to involve the local community in appreciation of, land use and landscape change. The aim was also to examine the impact of such change on the historic environment and to assess the implications for future land management. The intention is therefore to deliver this through a modular *'Archaeology, Landscape Change and Conservation'* project programme with a series of works in common between the different constituent projects.

A principal reason for promoting a programme of constituent projects rather than a single over-arching project has been in order to link up with local communities as partners in the process of exploring and conserving their local heritage. The intention is that a variety of local groups should be actively involved in these constituent projects across the county. At present, the aim is to develop a series of projects that where feasible are centred upon whole valleys such as the Arrow.

A series of broad objectives for these archaeology projects has therefore been closely defined:

1.   To assess the archaeological resource of the relevant part of the catchment (within LEADER+ parishes), using survey at a variety of scales

2.   To seek to reconstruct the recent landscape history of each area through detailed use of historic sources

3.   To gain some understanding of the long-term environmental history of each river valley through palaeoenvironmental investigations

4.   To investigate the dynamics of landscape change, and to improve knowledge of the local archaeology, through integrated site-specific studies

5.   To improve the management of archaeological sites and landscapes through a variety of activities, including site management works

6.   To share information about the historic environment of the areas concerned through a range of media

It is intended that in each constituent project the objectives will be addressed through a series of elements that will include:

· A profile of the local historic environment, based upon defined catchment areas and using a variety of sources including rapid terrain field-study

· An historical analysis of recent and more distant landscape development, using map regression and other analytical techniques

· Whole farm audits of visible historic landscape features, to include where possible detailed study of water management features

· An investigation of environmental history, employing geo-archaeological/palaeo-environmental consultants

· The mapping of landscape change and contemporary land-use impacts using a variety of sources including aerial photography and ground verification

· Selective recording and sample investigation of sites under active erosion, primarily in the arable landscape

· The provision of management advice for conservation (on a farm by farm basis, and via seminars)

· The conduct of practical conservation works, including site-based management action

· Provision of both wider-scale and site-specific interpretation information, materials and facilities

Each element of such a programme comprises a prospectus that, to provide anything approaching a comprehensive study, would take several years to complete. The aim of each project is therefore to 'make a start' and to show something of what can be done. The Arrow Valley project was a pilot study because it proposed an innovative way of surveying the landscape while at the same time engaging the community directly in a series of tasks and presentations. This resulted in the highly condensed time frame and timetable for the project.

The intention of the Archaeology, Landscape Change and Conservation project is clearly not therefore, to provide a once- and- for- all study of all the major river valleys in the county. Rather it sets out to explore some of the potential as well as trying to learn more about the historical development of each valley (and especially the river environs) from the time when people began to live here continuously after the last Ice Age 12,000 years ago up to the present day. It also aims to demonstrate the importance of the heritage of the landscape and settlements in the river valleys of Herefordshire, and to encourage others to explore it.

Finally, it is also important therefore to acknowledge that the Arrow Valley Archaeology, Landscape Change and Conservation project could only have happened with the help of the local community. In particular the farmers and landowners living in the Arrow Valley area have contributed enormously, and especially the Arrow Valley Farmers Group without whose enthusiasm many aspects of the project could not have been undertaken. Not only did they support the principles of the project but they also contributed their own time to it. Herefordshire Archaeology is grateful for their support and we hope this link will continue as a partnership in future projects and initiatives.

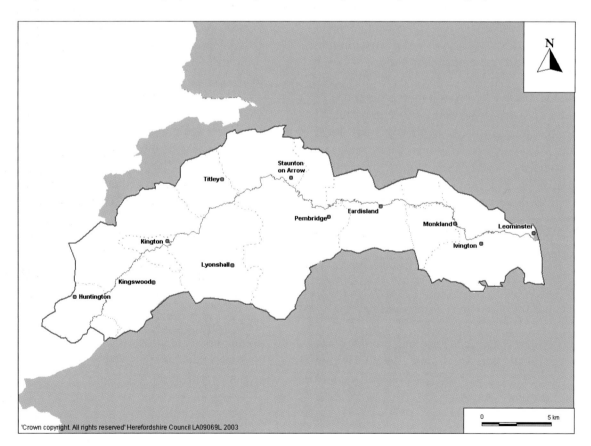

Figure 2 Location map of villages and parishes along the Arrow Valley

PART TWO

ARCHAEOLOGY

Chapter 2

An archaeological profile of the Arrow Valley

2.1 Archaeological information is a sample

The archaeology of all areas of Britain is important not least because it is often the only means we have to reach an understanding of what has happened in the past. Historical documents only refer to a small proportion of all human existence. Archaeology therefore is the only source available for the study of most of human history and archaeological remains are also important because of its their fragility. Once archaeological deposits have been destroyed they can never be recreated.

The question can then be posed as to how archaeology achieves this understanding of the past. Simply put, to begin to understand the history of any part of the landscape we need to do two things.

Firstly, we need to provide a 'framework' for such activity in time and space, using specifically archaeological methods of enquiry. We do this on the one hand by surveys to establish what can be learned across the landscape, about the locations used and the evidence left behind. On the other hand, we conduct site investigations that provide us with 'vignettes' – that is, information about cultural activity at a particular location, in some depth.

Secondly, we carry out 'complementary' studies in collaboration on the one hand with other scientists, local historians, and so on. On the other hand, we consult with local residents and landowners. What have they observed or retrieved over the years?

Since the history and archaeology of hardly any area of a country like England can be thought of as 'terra incognita' we need first to ask what we *knew* about the archaeology of the Arrow Valley at the start of 2003. The first port of call in such an enquiry is the county's Sites and Monument Record (SMR). Conveniently, the SMR for this county is also maintained by Herefordshire Archaeology, and is located in its offices in Hereford. (It is now also possible to consult the SMR online at www.smr.herefordshire.gov.uk).

In total there were by the beginning of 2003, 515 known sites or finds recorded in the SMR for the ten parishes along the Arrow Valley. These records represent sites or features that vary considerably in size, date and purpose. They range, for instance, from a single prehistoric flint implement to large medieval earthwork castles.

These distributions provide a clue to the current basis of information on the past (Figure 3). This information is mainly derived from random field observations, the chance discovery of objects, or (more rarely) from specific surveys of areas. It is important to understand the basis of such records a bit more closely.

For instance, a survey was carried out of the whole of Herefordshire at the end of the 19th century (Bevan *et al.,* 1896). This listed the bulk of the visible earthwork monuments then known. They were frequently the subject of visits by Victorian and Edwardian gentlemen (and sometimes ladies too), and were also the subject of antiquarian study and speculation reported on from 1851 onwards in the pages of the Transactions of the Woolhope Naturalists' Field Club.

At the same time, many of these more prominent sites had first been mapped by the surveyors of the Ordnance Survey at the end of the 18th century. So it was that they appeared with antique lettering on the first accurate maps of the whole landscape.

Then, in the 1930s, the Royal Commission on the Historical Monuments of England compiled a survey of the major monuments of the county, which they published in three volumes. The third of these volumes covered northwest Herefordshire (1934).

It is as a result of these early studies that some of the major monuments have come to enjoy protection under the law. Within these ten parishes there are therefore 20 Scheduled Ancient Monuments (SAMs). The purpose of designating and protecting these ancient monuments is discussed further in Chapter 9.

This rather small tally averaging two per parish includes 6 intermittent sections of Offa's Dyke, 5 motte and bailey castles, 4 mounds of varying size and description, 3 barrows, 2 hillforts, 1 moated site and a linear dyke system (Rowe Ditch) that traverses the river valley near Pembridge. It is perhaps worthwhile considering this 'sample' of sites in a little more detail, especially in light of what is discussed further below.

Firstly, these statutorily protected monuments represent less than 4% of the archaeological sites and features recorded in the Arrow Valley up until 2003. Secondly, they are all prominent earthwork monuments. Other less prominent sites have not been included. Thirdly, they represent in effect only two types of site – defensive sites or funerary monuments. No open settlements are included, even though sites as large as a whole deserted medieval settlement exist in two locations in the valley.

The 'sources' for the other known features are highly variable. So, for instance, of the 515 'known' sites, nearly half are in fact undated, or unassigned to any particular historical period. Why? Many of features are known from observations of earthworks seen in fields or from photography taken from the air. Often no further work in trying to understand these sites has been undertaken.

2.2 Arrow Valley history from archaeology, to 2003

Early activity

Since the end of the last Ice Age, nearly 12, 000 years ago, humans have left behind them artefacts,

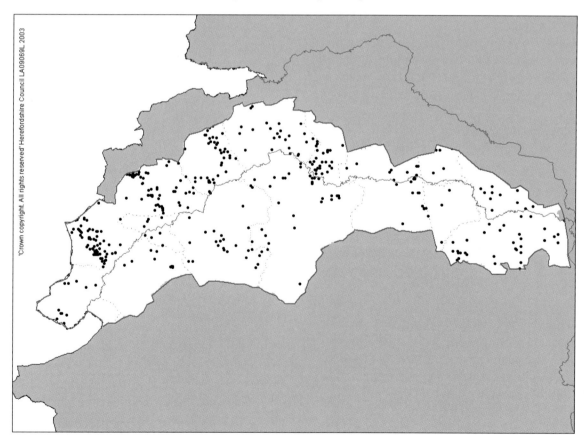

Figure 3 Distribution plot of known archaeological sites within the Arrow Valley to 2003

Period	Cropmarks	Earthworks	Other	Unclassified	Finds	Totals
Undated	70	103	0	0	3	176
Unknown	28	32	1 structure	0	0	61
Prehistoric	2	4	0	0	30	36
Palaeolithic	0	0	0	0	1	1
Mesolithic	0	0	0	0	3	3
Neolithic	0	0	0	0	4	4
Bronze Age	3	9	1 folklore	0	6	19
Iron Age	0	3	0	0	3	6
Roman	2	1	1 buried remains, 1 folklore	0	21	26
Saxon	0	12	2 buried remains	0	0	14
Early Medieval	0	2	0	0	0	2
Medieval	2	74	2 buried remains, 1 field system	1	11	91
Post Medieval	2	42	0	0	3	47
18th Century	0	2	0	0	0	2
19th Century	0	3	0	0	0	3
20th Century	0	1	0	0	0	1
Modern	0	21	0	0	0	21
1950	0	1	0	0	0	1
-	0	0	0	0	1	1
Totals	109	310	9	1	86	**515**

Table 1 Sites and Monuments Record data by type and period, known by 2003

evidence of settlements and burials that can inform us how they interacted with the landscape. This accumulation is what we have inherited in the landscape of the Arrow Valley today.

Isolated finds of Palaeolithic and Mesolithic implements have been noted within the river valley (Stamford, 1991; Dinn, 1999), but from the Neolithic onwards, the evidence for human activity is considerable. This is represented by the discovery of stone axes and worked flint implements especially in the area around Staunton and Pembridge. Although the working of flint is a sign of human occupation in the river valley (flint does not occur naturally in Herefordshire) this is often the only known evidence for prehistoric activity. No structures have ever been recovered arising from early prehistoric settlement although sites arising from how people in prehistory treated the dead and areas of possible ritual activity have survived to a limited extent.

Archaeological sites associated with the prehistoric period such as barrows and standing stones are recorded within the Arrow Valley. For example, Herefordshire's largest lowland barrow cemetery is located in the north of Pembridge parish, at Milton Cross. This comprises some five prominent barrows (three are Scheduled), and an equivalent number visible as surface spreads of material or as ring ditches in this area. Besides the Milton Cross barrow cemetery, other barrows are known or suspected in Titley, Eardisland, Kingsland and Leominster parishes. Standing stones have been reported (but not seen) at Huntington, and have been observed (previously noted as a 'mark' stone) at Lower Flintsham, Titley.

An axe-hammer and other stray finds of a bronze axe and a dagger provide the present artefactual evidence for Bronze Age activity. At the beginning of the 20th century a small hoard of Bronze Age spearheads were discovered at Broadward, Leominster, and these are now in the British Museum.

What is more certain is that there is substantial evidence for Iron Age activity in the valley and its margins. Major hillforts are located at Ivington Camp (Leominster) and Wapley Hill (Staunton-on-Arrow). In the valley itself, cropmarks indicate the presence of at least five likely farmstead enclosures.

Period	Pottery	Flint/ Stone	Coins	Metalwork	Findspot	Other	Totals
Undated	0	0	0	0	0	3	3
Prehistoric	0	30	0	0	0	0	30
Palaeolithic	0	1	0	0	0	0	1
Mesolithic	0	3	0	0	0	0	3
Neolithic	0	4	0	0	0	0	4
Bronze Age	0	2	0	4	0	0	6
Iron Age	0	0	3	0	0	0	3
Roman	15	0	4	1	0	1	21
Medieval	8	0	0	1	1	1	11
Post Medieval	2	0	0	0	0	1	3
-	0	0	0	0	0	1	1
Totals	25	40	7	6	1	7	86

Table 2 Sites and Monuments Record data by type of find known by 2003

Some of these clearly continued into (and may have begun life) in the Romano-British period.

First millennium AD

So far, no Roman forts or marching camps are known in the valley. The Roman Road, 'Watling Street West' however crosses the valley to the east of Eardisland (Figure 4). The suggestion has frequently been made locally that a Romano-British settlement existed at the crossing of the Stretford Brook. However it is perhaps equally likely that such a settlement may have existed at or near the crossing of the Arrow itself at Lawton east of Eardisland. Although there is no aerial photographic evidence to support the idea, some of the Romano-British farmsteads may have been connected to the main Roman Road by metalled 'side roads'. Apart from the Road, very few archaeological records for the Arrow Valley have been assigned to the Romano-British period. Roman period artefacts have been recovered in and around Staunton and Romano-British pottery has been found in fields around Ivington.

The archaeology of the later first millennium AD is represented first by Rowe Ditch, which is a straight linear earthwork that traverses the Arrow Valley from north to south on two distinct orientations just to the west of Pembridge. The bank is to the east with the ditch to the west, and the monument cuts across the landscape ignoring the earlier orientation of its fields and settlements. At least one Iron Age/ Romano-British earthwork directly underlies the dyke on that prior orientation. It seems likely that

this indicates a major cultural disjuncture, and the arrival of the Anglian population in the district sometime in the seventh century. No sites of this early period other than Rowe Ditch are known in the valley.

Offa's Dyke itself is a linear bank and ditch of yet more massive proportions but entirely different in character to Rowe Ditch. It enters the valley from Herrock Hill north of Kington, onto undulating fluvio-glacial terraces in the Titley area. It crosses the Arrow to the north of Lyonshall, pursuing a sinuous route southwards to pass west of the village, following the orientation of a further area of co-axial field system. Its date is presumed to be mid – eighth century.

The Normans and after

The eleventh century AD is represented most prominently by earthen (and formerly timber and stone) motte and bailey castles. Good examples of mottes are to be found in the upland areas, in Huntington (Turret Tump) and in Kington Rural (Castle Twts) parishes. Motte and bailey castles also survive in Huntington parish (Turret Castle and Huntington Castle). In the lowland areas, mottes are prominent by churches, at Staunton and Eardisland, for instance. Huntington developed into a curtain-walled castle, and these are present also at Lyonshall and (on a smaller scale) possibly also at the Court Farm moated site in Pembridge. Alongside these medieval defended sites were manorial sites, some of which were relatively rich, as has been shown by the quantity of imported

Figure 4 Aerial photograph of the Roman Road crossing the Arrow Valley at Eardisland. © HAAS 03-CN-0601

pottery of the twelfth century from excavations recently at Burton Court, Eardisland. Another 'lordly' site is present in the valley in the form of the Tironian Order medieval priory at Titley.

Medieval settlement is represented by sites of all scales, from medieval towns to rural townships and farmsteads. Several of each type of site are partly or wholly deserted. The former market towns include Kington (still a small market town) through Pembridge (a busy village on the A44), to Lyonshall (a major site formerly over a kilometre in linear extent, and now shrunken to a small village at the south end), to Huntington, which is almost entirely deserted. Villages range from Eardisland and Monkland (still modest settlements) through Titley (now a very dispersed settlement) to the disappeared villages of Ivington Green and Stretford. Hamlets or townships that are clearly deserted are known from aerial survey at Lawtonbury and Stagbatch (both in the western part of Leominster parish). Several of these smaller settlements are surrounded

by traces of their common fields either in the form of surviving ridge and furrow (Lawtonbury has a particularly rich group), or fossilised in the form of the later hedgerows and field boundaries.

Post-medieval settlements are obviously difficult to distinguish from earlier ones, though industrial sites are more evident. The valley is particularly rich in mills, the Glanarrow Mill complex at Eardisland being an outstanding survival, and more 'archaeological' remains being those for instance at Arrow Green by Lawton. Also at Lawton is the remains of a rural industrial complex to the west of Lawtonbury Farm, while the remains of another such complex may survive at The Forge, Staunton.

Past archaeological fieldwork

There have been no major excavations within the Arrow Valley, although during the late 1970s and early 1980s, David Hill of Manchester University Extra Mural Department excavated several trenches across the presumed northern end of Rowe Ditch. This formed part of the investigation of linear dyke systems in the Welsh Marches (Hill and Worthington, 2003). The excavations revealed that although the earthwork was no longer extant above ground to the north of the scheduled earthwork, Rowe Ditch would have originally continued northwards, as the quarry ditch appeared to survive to well over 1.80m in depth. However it was not fully investigated during the fieldwork project concerned.

In 1991 the former county archaeological service for Hereford and Worcester, commissioned by English Heritage, undertook the Marches Upland Survey within Herefordshire and Shropshire. The survey involved twenty 1km wide transects, located in the upland zone along the Welsh Border, ten transects were in Herefordshire. The southern most areas of three transects (Nash, Hergest Ridge and Herrock Hill) included land within the Arrow Valley parishes. The study included a review of the existing SMR records, checking of available aerial photography and field walking within each transect. The number of known sites in each transect increased between seven and twenty-five times, following the study. This survey was limited in topographic extent to the upland landscape, but it did demonstrate both the general potential and the conditions under which archaeological features survive (Dinn, 1995a,b,c; Dinn and Edwards, 1999). One form of discovery that has in recent years increased our knowledge of archaeological sites, river deposits and the formation of the landscape is aerial photography. This is also important because it helps to provide a framework for landscape-scale investigation. Some mapping was undertaken from exisitng photographs during the Marches Upland Survey as part of the then RCHM(E) National Mapping Programme.

The former county archaeological service also conducted the Central Marches Historic Towns Survey in the area in the 1990s, with funding from English Heritage. The settlements at Leominster, Pembridge and Huntington were the subject of reports that identified the possible plan form components and summarised what was known. Lyonshall was not recognised at the time as a medieval urban settlement (Ray, 2001).

2.3 Information from aerial photography, to 2003

Archaeologists increasingly use aerial photography as a tool to study the archaeology and landscape of an area. It is a very important tool as it can provide, literally, a new perspective on a site or landscape you are looking at. The use of air borne reconnaissance to record and discover archaeological sites is not new however. Aerial photographers Keith St. Joseph and Arnold Baker were flying over the Arrow Valley during the late 1950s and into the 1970s respectively. Their photography focused on the most obvious features in the landscape- Rowe Ditch, the hilllforts, the line of the Roman road and the various castles along the river valley.

This earlier photography is still very useful as it can provide an indication of how the landscape and archaeological sites have changed during the latter part of the 20th century. Two examples of change to historical sites from opposite ends of the Arrow Valley demonstrate this. At Ivington Camp archive photography from 1960s show the ramparts of the hillfort under pasture and rough grazing. Today it is now a woodland landscape specialising in game shoots (Figure 5). Where the Arrow enters the county Huntington Castle is now largely overgrown but aerial photography from the 1980s show the area of the motte and bailey under grazed pasture.

Figure 5   Ivington Camp, Leominster from the east. ©HAAS 03-CN-0918

Exploration of the wider landscape followed during the 1970s and 1980s with photography undertaken by Jim Pickering and more recently by Chris Musson who has been involved in the most recent aerial survey, up to 2003, in identifying and recognising sites in the Arrow Valley. This was part of a wider programme of flying across the county as part of the Millennium Air Survey of Herefordshire sponsored by The Field Names Survey of the Woolhope Naturalists' Field Club and supported by English Heritage and Herefordshire Archaeology.

The time of year that aerial photography is undertaken is important, as different types of historical features will show better at different times. During the winter months, earthworks such as ridge and furrow, former field boundaries and water leats will show up well because of the angle of the sun upon the earthworks. During the summer months, buried archaeology will show either as parch marks in grass or as a cropmark within an arable field.

An important point to appreciate, is that for a site to be recognised as a cropmark, it must be under erosion from ploughing. It is a considerable irony therefore that its discovery is linked to its destruction. An aspect of this project was to assess, through limited investigations, the potential rate of erosion on some different types of site.

At present there are one hundred and nine cropmark sites (as recorded in the SMR) recognisable from aerial photography in the Arrow Valley. Many of these sites are situated in the fertile, lowland areas of the river valley. There are rectangular shaped cropmarks recorded around Kington, Lyonshall and Titley. These may represent enclosed farmsteads that date to the later prehistoric or Romano- British period.

Further along the river valley from Staunton-on-Arrow, through Pembridge to Eardisland a variety of cropmark sites have been recorded. Many of these appear as groups or clusters of circular cropmarks of varying sizes known as ring ditches (Figure 6). These sites represent prehistoric activity in the form of burial and funerary areas for the interment of people beneath earthen monuments. The ditches were dug to demarcate a circular funerary area, and to provide soil for the covering mound. The density

of these ring ditches can be high. Around Milton Cross, for example, there are more than twenty of these ring ditches or prehistoric artefact spreads that have been recorded as well as the Scheduled Ancient Monuments of the barrow cemetery noted above.

Further groups of ring ditches and enclosures are recorded to the south of Leominster and on the interfluve between the River Arrow and the Stretford Brook. However, it is not just man- made features that show up as cropmarks and can provide an indication of other more deeply buried remains. Differences in crop colour can also reveal environmental features such as the former river channels along the river valley. These are of interest as the wet silts of a former channel may contain organic material, such as plants, animal remains and seeds, that can inform us about the earlier environment and ecology of an area. Such differences may also indicate an area of human activity associated with the water channel that may not as yet have been recognised. In other cases the actual relationship between the archaeology and former river channels can be observed from such aerial photography. This has led us to think about the possibilities of investigating such sites especially where there is the opportunity to understand the relationship between archaeological sites and the movement of the river.

Figure 6 Cropmarks of ring ditches, east of Eardisland. © CPAT 90-C-231

2.4 A recent phase of archaeological exploration

Although before 1998, there had been little exploration of the Arrow Valley landscape, since then the aerial work by Chris Musson as part of the Millennium Air Survey of Herefordshire has been complemented by localised work that has identified new sites, and has involved some limited investigation of key sites and areas.

An example is the Eardisland Oral History Group's investigations of the environs of Burton Court, one of the three manors of medieval Eardisland. The group have explored the cellars of the main house (which features the remains of a fourteenth century hall). They have also surveyed the surroundings of the house, and have investigated a garden landscaping mound that preserved underneath it midden deposits from the early manor (Selfe, 2002).

Members of staff from Herefordshire Archaeology have noted features in the course of their work. This has included the recognition of the earthworks of the medieval town of Lyonshall (Ray, 2001), but also the suggestion that the place-name 'Lawton' may refer to the Anglo-Saxon 'Leaw-tun', or 'settlement by the mound', and that this may be marked by a vestigial barrow at Lawton Cross. (Ray, pers. comm). The earthworks of a likely deserted medieval settlement at Lawtonbury were noted from the ground during a Countryside Stewardship site visit to Lawtonbury in 1999 (Ray, pers. comm and Herefordshire Archaeology files).

Lyonshall has recently become the focus for a Cardiff University based research project looking at the Herefordshire countryside in the Romano-British period (Guest, forthcoming). Aerial photography is also continuing, with the Herefordshire Aerial Archaeological Survey project supported by Herefordshire Council and English Heritage. Chris Musson is involved with this project, with recording also by Paul White and Tim Hoverd of Herefordshire Archaeology.

Chapter summary: some key points

- There are over 500 sites and monuments recorded in the parish group along the Arrow Valley

- Over half of these sites are not yet attributed to any specific historical period

- Recent survey and aerial photography have increased our knowledge of the overall distribution of archaeological sites but not their purpose and relationship to the wider landscape

- Although cropmarks are discovered by ploughing, the process of ploughing gradually destroys the archaeological deposits and sites

Chapter 3

Earlier prehistory from project fieldwork

3.1   Introduction

It is clear from the review of existing information in Chapter 2 that evidence for activity in earlier prehistory (taken here as the period through to the end of the Bronze Age, c.800 BC) mainly comes from stray finds and objects. This project provided the opportunity to investigate in more detail the nature of prehistoric activity in the Arrow Valley.

The opportunity was also seen to exist, to try to develop a *parallel* understanding of the activity of the river itself (geomorphological study) as well as of the peoples who lived close to it (archaeology). So it was that some of the sites chosen for investigation because of the cropmarks that appeared indicative of early settlement, were also chosen because of the apparently close association with indications of past river channel activity.

The ephemeral nature of activity before 4,000 BC was highlighted by a find made in 2002 during archaeological excavations as part of the Cardiff University research project looking at the origins and development of farming settlements in the Lyonshall area. What appeared to be a natural hollow was found, filled with wind-blown or water-borne sand. This was found only because it was located (coincidentally) within a later enclosure (Peter Guest, pers comm). This hollow was excavated by the Cardiff team, and produced a small assemblage of microliths. These are tiny flint objects used in composite artefacts during the Mesolithic period (c.10,000-4,000 BC). What this find tells us is that small bands of people living a nomadic hunting and collecting-based lifestyle had made a small temporary encampment in the area.

In contrast, the 'visibility' of early communities increases markedly from the Neolithic and Bronze Ages (from c. 4000 BC), when the peoples who inhabited the area had begun to create the kind of constructions that are more readily visible to archaeological investigation.

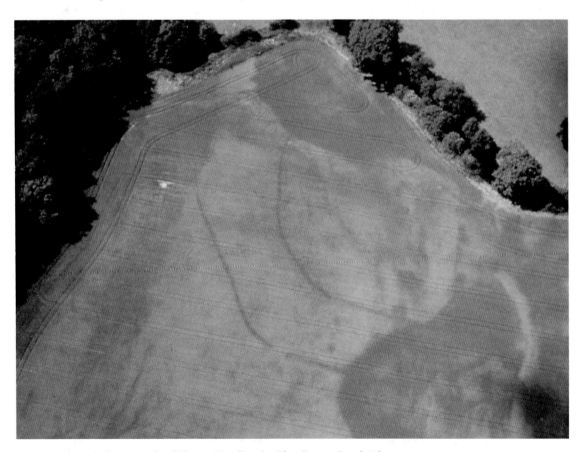

Figure 7 Aerial photograph of Upper Headlands, The Grove, Pembridge. ©CPAT MASH 96-C-1574

3.2 Upper Headlands, The Grove, Staunton-on-Arrow (GRO 03): the later Neolithic

Reasons for investigation

The site at The Grove, Staunton-on-Arrow was chosen for investigation for two reasons. Firstly, aerial photography in 1996 (96-MB-0514 to 96-MB-0516) had revealed that in a field just to the south of the Arrow, there were traces of two concentric lengths of ditch aligned broadly east-west and separated by around 30 metres (Figure 7). This

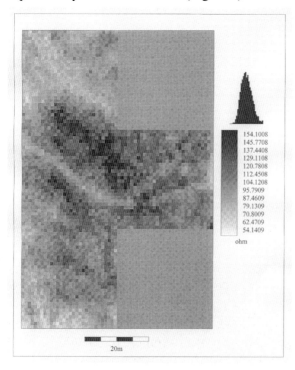

Figure 8 Resistivity results at Upper Headlands

indicated the possibility that a former (and presumably early) enclosure had been deliberately located close to the river here.

Secondly, this site was located at a point where the river emerged from a narrow section of valley to the west, into a less constrained area in which deposition of silts had taken place, just to the northeast of the parish focus at the church. However, the series of aerial photographs also revealed that there was some complexity to river development here, since there were clearly silted-up past stream channels immediately adjacent to the site in question – and indeed surrounding it to both east and west.

There was another particular reason to be interested in this site, from an archaeological perspective. This was because of the form of the ditches, and their configuration. Simply put, they appeared most likely to be like straightforward enclosure ditches. As cut, these would have been open to the sky. They would have been used for drainage, to keep stock out, and possibly also for defence. In the case of the outer of the two ditches there was apparently an entrance way, with an interruption in the ditch where a gateway could have stood.

However, they could also, given their apparent narrowness, be 'read' instead as palisade trenches. This would mean that in reality they had been 'fence' lines, with the 'fence' in this case potentially being a line of oak posts set vertically into the ground, that might have stood several metres high when first built.

Now if this was the case, there were parallels with sites in the Avebury area in Wiltshire, and further afield, where such 'palisades' enclosed oval-shaped areas in the later Neolithic (c.3000-2200BC). In the Scottish Borders at Meldon Bridge, a more widely spaced palisade had been found that had actually cut off a promontory between two rivers. There was however a good parallel very much closer at hand, where two such palisades had been shown to define separate massive oval enclosures at Walton and at Hindwell, only ten kilometres to the west of Staunton (Gibson, 1999).

So, interest in the site was focused upon the idea that it might feature remains from the Neolithic period. In the event, this did indeed prove more or less to be the case – but not for the reasons that in part led the site to be studied in the first place.

The site investigations

The site investigations of May 2003 did provide insights into the nature of the enclosure at Upper Headlands, and to the date of each of the two ditches. A series of five trenches were opened at the site, to investigate what had appeared in the 1996 aerial photographs. However, this site work was also informed by a geophysical survey carried out by Herefordshire Archaeology staff immediately before the excavations began in May 2003.

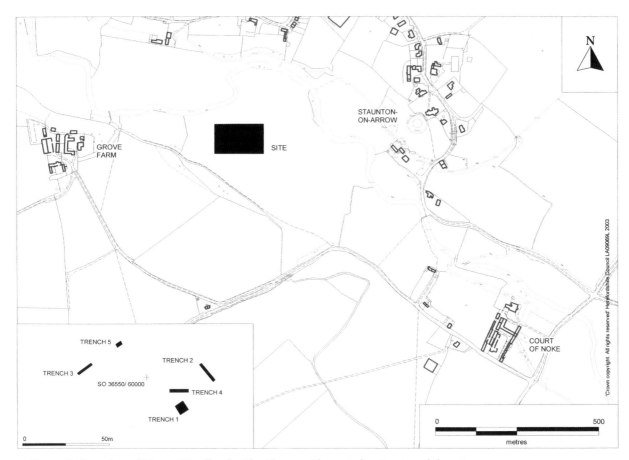

Figure 9 Location of Upper Headlands, The Grove with inset showing trench locations

Firstly, the location of the two lengths of ditch apparent on the aerial photographs was located directly on the ground. The field was once subdivided, but now there are no boundaries between Nokehead Lane to the south and the present bank of the Arrow to north and east. However, the wooded slope that rises towards The Grove to the west is differentiated along its length, and this helped locate the cropmark feature positions. Moreover, the larger areas of darker green that appeared in the ripening crop in 1996 conformed closely to areas of substantially lower ground actually *within* the field. So it was possible to define a zone for examination that approximated reasonably well to the 'target' area for close investigation.

The purpose of the geophysical survey across this area was then twofold. Firstly, it would enable the pinpointing of the course of the two ditches on the ground. Secondly, it might provide indications of the presence of further features ancillary to, or entirely different from, the lines already noted from the air under optimal conditions in 1996.

Conditions in 2003 were far from ideal for observing anything on the ground, since the field was under grass. Nonetheless, this did mean that the site could be investigated without undue disturbance to a growing crop. Mr. Austin Owens is to be thanked here, as elsewhere in this report, for his co-operation in making the site available in this way, and for his visits with his family to see the progress of work.

The geophysics presented a picture that did augment the aerial view just as had been intended. The Geoscan RM105 twin-probe resistivity instrument used for the survey sends a small electric charge into the soil. Areas of greater or lesser resistance to this current provide a signal that enables such areas to be distinguished from those around them.

The survey showed up the lines of both the inner and outer enclosure ditches (Figure 8). However, the survey also traced the western edge of a separate feature, apparently leading northwards from the northern side of part of the southern-most of the two ditch circuits. It was not apparent from the survey whether this 'new' feature actually cut across the ditch, or was contemporary with it (or was indeed later in date).

The excavation was therefore designed in part to clarify this relationship, as well as to investigate the course of both circuits of ditch. The first trench opened was located at the apparent entrance- way across the outer circuit of ditch (Figure 9). The second trench was cut across the line of the outer ditch on the 'opposite side' of the entrance- way examined in Trench 1. It was also located so as to intercept the feature revealed on the eastern edge of the geophysical survey.

Trench 3 was sited over the line of the inner circuit of ditch. The fourth trench was cut between the two circuits, to see if any features survived in the 'interior' of the enclosure. The fifth trench was cut within the innermost circuit, for the same reason.

Results and site interpretation: a 'Beaker' settlement?

The excavations effectively disproved that the ditches were palisades, and moreover gave a strong indication that they dated from the Iron Age. As a

consequence, the findings related to these features will be discussed further in the next chapter.

What was discovered in Trench 2 did however open up an entirely new dimension to the site at Upper Headlands, The Grove. This was because it was possible during the excavation to reveal a clear and unambiguous relationship between the outer ditch of the enclosure shown in the aerial photographs, and the feature revealed in the geophysical survey. In short, the former cut through the latter, which continued southwards from the point of intersection (Figure 10).

The true nature of this linear feature however, remains ambiguous. This is because, although it was shown to have three distinctly different fills, no eastern side to the feature was found. This enables us to discount the idea that this might itself be a simple ditch – unless it is very broad.

The lowest of the three fills of this feature contained no surviving cultural items. In other words no artefacts were recovered from within the area excavated. However, the upper two fills produced a piece of burnt flint and several small sherds of

Figure 10 Photograph of Trench 2 showing the earlier feature, aligned along the length of the trench, being cut by the outer enclosure ditch from left to right

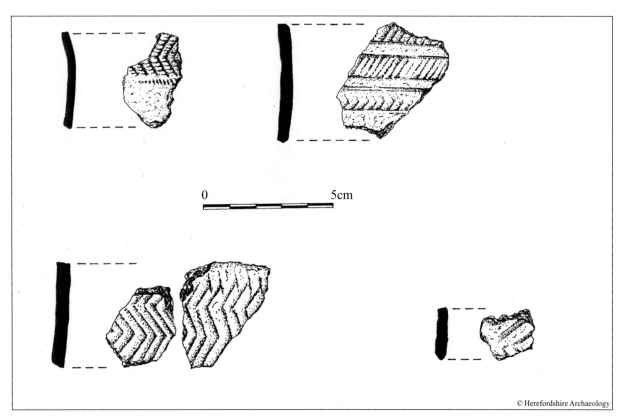

*Figure 11 Drawing of the fragments of Beaker pottery retrieved from Upper Headlands, The Grove. (Drawing by
T.Hoverd)*

'Beaker' pottery (Figure 11). This immediately indicates a date for this phase of activity, to the late Neolithic or very early Bronze Age (see *Appendix 1*). The period pinpointed by comparison with finds elsewhere is 2300-1700 BC, with a slight preference (with substantial caveats) for the later part of this range.

Beaker pottery is very distinctive, especially where, as at this site, there is comb-impressed or incised decoration in bands. The vessels belonging to this tradition are thin-walled, and, as the name used by archaeologists suggests, they are like cups without handles (although a very few are also found with single handles). Beaker vessels do vary in size from around 10 to 30 cms and sometimes more in height. They vary even more in shape and decorative scheme. What exactly they were used for is uncertain, but the drinking of alcoholic beverages is indicated in cases where traces of a mead-like liquid have been traced from chemical analysis of their interior surfaces.

The Beaker sherds concerned here come from four vessels, each of which had a different decorative scheme. In Herefordshire, there have been a number

of finds of such pottery, although much of it has simpler decoration. Moreover, most finds have been of individual vessels, and have clearly come from funerary contexts. This is as an accompaniment to a person buried in a pit or stone box with other grave goods. An example is the particularly fine example found in 1996 at Wellington Quarry on the river Lugg with a poorly preserved skeleton, fine flint arrowheads, a fragment of a polished wristguard, and a small copper dagger (Harrison, Jackson and Napthan, 1999).

There are a number of potentially significant things that the present discovery of these Beaker sherds tells us. Firstly, there was clearly activity right at the base of the river valley, possibly on the edges of the river channel as it was then, in the later Neolithic period perhaps through to the late Bronze Age (see Chapter 5).

However, its existence in the upper fills of a (presumably) man-made feature adds to the significance of the find. This suggests a deposit of definite 'structure' (that is, a feature cut by tools into the natural alluvium) that was created as a result of settlement activity (at least for the burial of midden material). By definition, this feature as originally cut, was created *before* the period represented by the upper fills that contained the Beaker pottery.

What this suggests is that the feature intercepted by the later ditches at Upper Headlands, The Grove, represents a perhaps periodic riverside settlement that belongs to an earlier and a later Neolithic phase of activity, continuing on into the Bronze Age.

Significance

The significance of the discovery of late Neolithic/ Beaker activity by the River Arrow between Staunton and Pembridge is considerable. Firstly, it is the only evidence yet obtained for apparently 'domestic' Beaker activity in the county, although some of the evidence for Wellington suggests that midden deposits may have been deposited near the River Lugg there, at around the same time (Jackson, forthcoming).

A further significance is to be found in the fact that this material was deposited so close to the river. What this clearly indicates is that, at least by the end of the Neolithic (c. 2000 BC) there was much activity specifically related to the river. We know from aerial photographic evidence that much of this activity, represented by ring ditches, is likely to have been ceremonial or funerary in character (see below). While we have noted an apparently domestic nature to this activity, the proximity to the river could mean that the midden itself might be a votive deposit.

3.3 Top Hales, The Leen Farm, Pembridge (LTH 03): the early Bronze Age

Reasons for investigation

As noted above, in the area between the River Arrow and the roads at Milton Cross there is an abundance of ring ditches recorded from aerial photography (Figure 12). There are more than twenty of these cropmark sites located around Rowe Ditch in Pembridge. These circular cropmarks are usually thought to represent the ditches dug around burial mounds or barrows that were most likely constructed during the prehistoric period, from the late Neolithic to the mid- Bronze Age. When these

Figure 12 Aerial photograph of ring ditches and associated archaeological features at Milton Cross.
©CPAT 90-C-164

sites have not been ploughed in historically recent times, they continue to survive as mounds within modern fields. In fact the best example of surviving barrows in Herefordshire are at Milton Cross itself. Normally at the centre of the ring ditch or barrow is the primary burial that is then covered by the up-cast of the quarry ditches dug in a circle around the burial. Sometimes further burials (often in the form of a cremation) are interred into the edges of the barrow implying that people over several generations were being buried next to or as close as possible to their illustrious predecessor.

Ring ditches can range from 8 metres to over 20 metres in diameter and are sometimes located in groups considered by archaeologists to be a type of cemetery. This all suggests that areas of the prehistoric landscape were reserved specifically for the dead and that special respect was given to the ancestors in these defined areas.

One aspect of the barrow construction is that the up-cast soil for the mound has sealed the land surface as it was at the time of its construction. This is of special interest to archaeologists as it is possible to study through excavation the prehistoric land surfaces and associated features that elsewhere have been lost through ploughing and landscape change since the prehistoric period.

On the northern edge of the River Arrow a site provided an opportunity to investigate two cropmark ring ditches. Within the Top Hales field at least three such ditched features have been observed from aerial photography. The largest ring ditch (over 16 metres in diameter) was selected for investigation because of its close topographic relationship to a former channel of the Arrow (Figures 13 and 14).

The western side of the ring ditch disappeared into an area of wet silts deposited by the river channel. This raised the question of which came first. If the ring ditch was the earliest feature, had the river channel buried the archaeology under deep silt deposits that might contain important organic material? Alternatively had the river eroded the archaeological feature?

To the south of this ring ditch was an unusual feature. Rather than a circular ring ditch this feature was more of an oval shape. It was unclear whether this was earlier, contemporary or later than the ring ditch. However, such oval ditched features have proved in other parts of Britain to have been constructed during the Neolithic period.

The investigations at Top Hales had three aims. The first aim was to determine the relationship between the archaeological deposits and the river channel. The second aim was to retrieve dating evidence from the archaeological deposits in order to confirm the date of the cropmarks. The third aim was to assess whether any buried soils survived under the up-cast from the quarry ditches.

The site investigations

As with Upper Headlands at The Grove the area of darker green that appeared in the ripening crop in 1996 conformed closely to areas of substantially lower ground actually *within* the field (Figure 13). The extent of the former river meander could therefore be defined clearly on the ground. Both of the cropmarks are situated upon what appears to be a west-facing slope within the field. It was possible to locate the trenches from the topography and to calculate the distance from the surrounding field boundaries by measurements derived from the aerial photograph. Following the removal of a cereal crop in August 2003 two trenches were excavated in Top Hales. The first trench measured 10m x 12.5m and was located over the western end of the oval shaped cropmark. The second trench was located in the southwest quadrant of the ring ditch and measured 9.5m x 10m (Figure 15).

This latter trench was sited primarily to determine the relationship between the archaeology and the river channel. A mechanical digger was used to

Figure 13 Aerial photograph of the cropmarks at Top Hales, The Leen Farm, Pembridge.

excavate the upper deposits (ploughsoil), but care was taken to ensure that no obvious damage occurred to the possible up-cast material within the circuit of both ditches. This meant the excavation team had to spend time subsequently cleaning back the site so that the archaeological deposits could become clarified.

Results and site interpretation: a story of erosion

The trenches revealed that the eastern sides of the ring ditch archaeological features, located on the slightly higher ground were less than 30 cm below the top of the ploughsoil. It appears that any remnants of a mound have been removed. Moreover the possibility that any buried soils might survive beneath the up-cast of the mound is also regarded as remote.

Trench 1

In Trench 1, focused upon the oval ditch, two cross sectional areas (termed 'slots' here) were excavated through the ditch (Figure 16). One was located at the eastern side of the trench and the other one on the northern side. The excavations showed that the ditch had been excavated through the underlying natural gravels by prehistoric people, and the up-cast placed within the circuit of the ditch. This could be determined in this way because the gravel excavated out of the ditch had slumped back into it at some point in the remote past and the ditch had then gradually silted up. As noted above, the morphology suggests that this oval shaped feature may be a barrow possibly dating to the Neolithic period. Unfortunately no artefacts were recovered from either of these slots excavated across the ditch to support or contradict this possibility.

The absence of artefacts on the site was nonetheless compensated for by the complexity of the archaeological deposits examined. The eastern most section across the ditch revealed that this was not the first human activity on the site as the ditch cut through the back filled deposit of a large pit. A band of fine dark silt was revealed at the western end of the trench and corresponds with the line of the former river channel.

Trench 2

This same silt deposit was also observed in Trench 2 but to a greater extent. Almost the entire western half of Trench 2 was covered by this fine silt which made tracing the location of the ditch very difficult. It was decided that four slots should be excavated

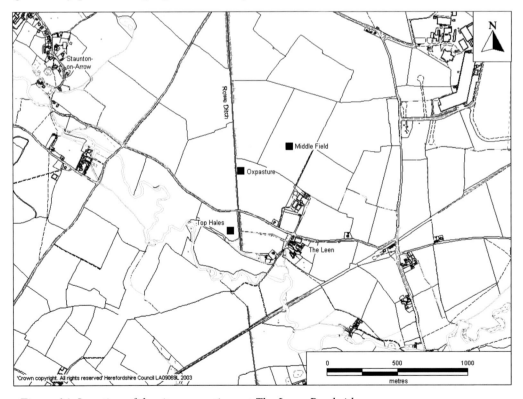

Figure 14 Location of the site excavations at The Leen, Pembridge

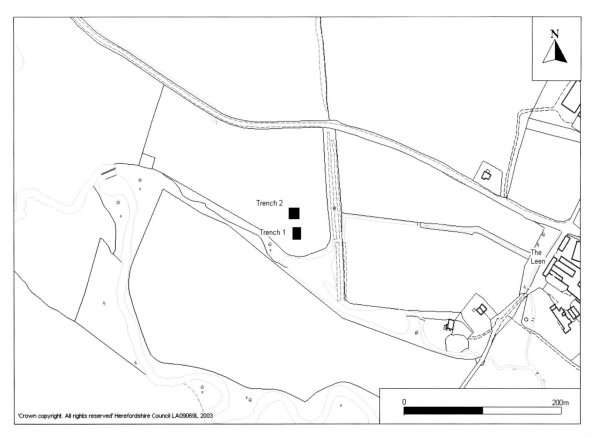

Figure 15 Location of trenches at Top Hales, The Leen, Pembridge

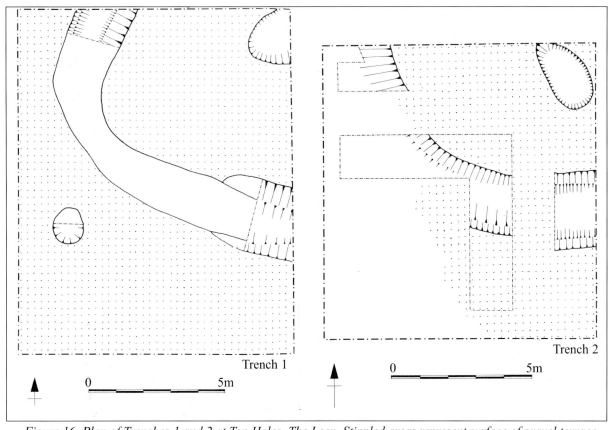

Figure 16 Plan of Trenches 1 and 2 at Top Hales, The Leen. Stippled areas represent surface of gravel terrace and blank areas represent silts or ditch/ feature fills

across the ring ditch to determine its profile, retrieve any artefacts and establish its relationship to the river channel (Figure 16).

The first slot across the ditch revealed that a mound had existed on the inside of the ditch circuit and this had to some extent slipped back into the quarry ditch just as in the case of the oval ditched feature. The ditch then gradually silted up completely.

The profile of the ditch was confirmed by the second slot excavated next to the first. However, it was the other two slots across the western edge of the ring ditch that revealed its full history.

These two slots showed that the river channel had eroded the western edge of the ditch almost entirely away (Figure 17). In the northern slot no remains of the ditch survived but in the next slot the very bottom of the primary gravel fills of the ditch could be seen overlain by the deposition of silt from the river channel.

This proved that the ring ditch feature, or barrow, had been constructed before the water channel eroded this area of river bank. But when did the erosion occur? As with the oval ring ditch, no artefacts were recovered from the fill of this circular ring ditch.

Within the upper silt levels of the river deposits were found very small, abraded pieces of Romano-British pottery. These fragments included early types of Severn Valley wares and a piece of Samian pottery, imported from the Continent from the mid-first to mid- third century AD. The size and abraded nature of the pottery suggests that the pottery is not evidence for Roman activity on the site itself but perhaps it was washed from another site upstream or nearby, and was then deposited in the river silts over the ring ditch.

It also suggests that the river channel at this location expanded at some point during the Roman Period, or perhaps slightly earlier, and that this resulted in the site becoming eroded away, at least in part.

Although no artefacts were recovered from the deposits within the ring ditch following cleaning of the trench, a small oval pit was discovered in the north- eastern corner of the trench. This pit was situated within the south- western quarter of the area

Figure 17 Trench 2 looking east. The truncated western side of the ring ditch due to river channel change is clearly visible

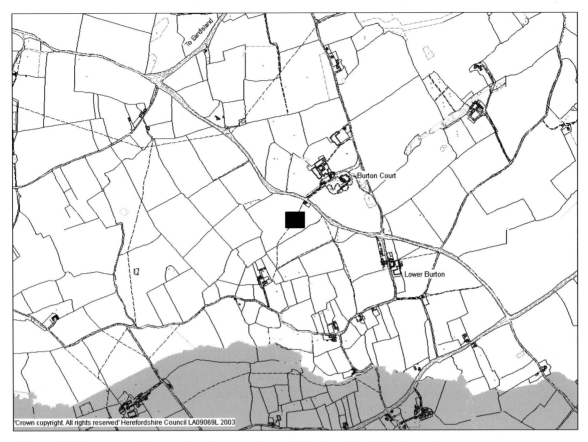

Figure 18 Location of the investigations at Admarsh Meadow, Eardisland

enclosed by the ditch. The pit contained over thirty pieces of knapped flint, possibly of later Neolithic date. The pit appears to have been dug into the subsoil here before the mound had been raised within the circular ditch.

Significance

This site confirms the existence of early prehistoric activity within the river valley near to the river channel. The proximity of the sites to each other also suggests a complexity and density of activity in the low-lying areas of the Arrow Valley. The discovery of the pit containing flint may imply that there is also some potential for discovering earlier archaeological features buried beneath these sites, that survive to a varying degree.

The recovery of very abraded Romano- British pottery in the silts of the river channel may suggest a date when this phase of erosion took place and this may support the interpretation of the geomorphological survey that there was a phase of flooding during the first four hundred years of the first millennium AD (see Chapter 6; Macklin *et al*).

3.4 Admarsh, Eardisland (WHE 03): the middle Bronze Age

Reasons for the investigation

In 2000 Bronze Age metalwork was discovered at Admarsh, Eardisland. A local history enthusiast using a metal detector had been walking along the up-cast of a former drainage channel and had discovered a short bladed knife or dirk. This discovery was reported to Herefordshire Archaeology, and the Arrow Valley project in 2003 provided an opportunity to investigate the area around the discovery.

Evidence for the Bronze Age is scant for the entire county so the possibility of investigating a site of this period could not be ignored. No Bronze Age settlement structures have been discovered in the county and evidence for the period from 1400 BC to 1000 BC is based almost entirely upon the discovery and reporting of metalwork finds across the county. No such sites have ever been systematically investiagted in Herefordshire so soon after the discoveries concerned were made.

35

Within the Arrow Valley this is the fourth recorded find of Bronze Age metalwork. At the turn of the 20th century a hoard of socketed bronze spearheads was discovered at Broadward as noted in Chapter 2 (section 2.2) above. These objects are now in the British Museum. A Bronze Age dagger was found near a pond in Lyonshall parish and is now in Hereford Museum . More recently a bronze axe also from near Lyonshall has been reported to Herefordshire Archaeology but this has not yet been substantiated. The discovery of metalwork is often associated with agricultural works such as ploughing or the cutting of drainage ditches. The location of these finds from around Britain suggests that the original deposition was often into wet or waterlogged areas and fulfilled an important ritual purpose.

The site investigations

This discovery at Admarsh had the potential to reveal a previously unknown site of Bronze Age activity, in an area suggested by its name to be potentially waterlogged. There was a possibility that organic material might survive provided an adequate stimulus in addition to concerns that other material deposited at the same time might be found. Twelve small trenches would be excavated across the field around the location of the discovery to assess the deposits (Figure 18). Most of these trenches were focused around the area identified as near to the

findspot, but three test pits were also excavated on the higher ground of the hillslope to the west in an attempt to discover any possible prehistoric features that might relate to a settlement that once could have existed here. The test pits were excavated by hand and the soil sieved by an excavation team comprising of members of the Eardisland Oral History Group, who are undertaking archaeological investigations at Burton Court. We are grateful to the landowner, Mr. Watkins, for permitting the excavation to take place. Local testimony obtained by the Eardisland Group members indicated that the character of this field has changed markedly in recent years (see below).

Results and site interpretations: a prehistoric ritual deposit

As soon as the first three trenches had been opened and excavated it became clear that no organic material was likely to have survived here. The subsoil consisted of fine grey coloured clay- silt which is diagnostic of sedimentation from low velocity water movement. Liaison with the geomorphology team from Aberystwyth University confirmed the absence of any organic material from the coring samples that they took across the site. The excavation and coring suggested that the area was an area of seasonal flooding that probably produced a seasonal water-filled pond but consisted

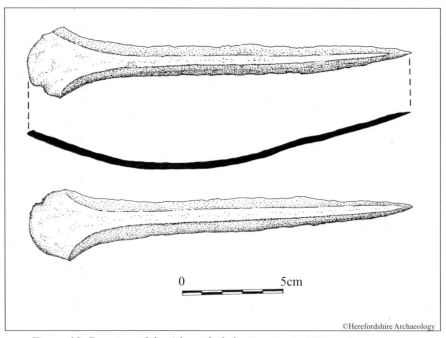

0 _____ 5cm

©Herefordshire Archaeology

Figure 19 Drawing of the Admarsh dirk. (Drawing by T.Hoverd)

of fairly free flowing water as there was very little organic material with the deposit.

No further prehistoric artefacts were recovered from the excavation. Fragments of post- medieval pottery were recovered from the topsoil and the only features to be discovered were the remains of stone lined drains, at least 0.5 metres below the ground surface.

The trenches located on the slopes were excavated to a substantial depth through layers of clay and sandy silts. This suggested that recent hillwash was prevalent at the site. The Oral History Group confirmed this when local residents were asked about the site and people recalled that the slopes and hilltop to the west had been a coppice until the 1970s. This was then was bulldozed and cleared for pasture.

Although the discovery of the dirk is evidence for Middle Bronze Age activity it remains the only evidence we have from Admarsh for the prehistoric period. But what can we learn from studying the dirk itself?

A leading expert on Bronze Age metalwork, Dr. Martyn Barber, has examined the piece and has provided some interesting insights (*Appendix 2*). The blade appears to have been bent deliberately, before it was deposited (Figure 19). It seems to have been a finished piece of metalwork but there is no indication that it was ever hafted on a handle. It is believed to date to around 1400 –1140 BC. Dating of these types of metalwork is difficult for two reasons. Firstly, the majority of metalwork that is recorded has been retrieved in a similar way through serendipity. The result, apart from the discovery of the metalwork, is the removal of the artefact from its buried context and any associated artefacts that may aid dating. Secondly dating is very difficult because no one dirk is the same - each was made from a single mould so any comparison of the metalwork form is relative and based upon assumptions about typology (the inference of chronological and cultural significance of differences in form).

Significance

Again, although we have learned little about middle Bronze Age settlement activity from the investigation of the context of this find, there are several points of significance to be highlighted.

Firstly, the fact that this was a seasonally water-filled deposit indicates the kind of environmental variety that existed in these interfluve areas.

Secondly, such areas were likely to have been relatively remote from settlement. This was an area that could have been the abode of gods and spirits – somewhere appropriate for the making of votive offerings of precious objects.

Thirdly, something of the wealth of these local communities is indicated by their preparedness to deposit fine objects using scarce materials. The likelihood is that this dagger had never been hafted. It was likely therefore to have been made specifically for the act of deposition that took place here.

Chapter summary: some key points

■ The discovery of a Beaker period site is very important, especially if this is a location for settlement in the later Neolithic (c. 2500- 2000 BC).

■ Ditched funerary monuments appear to have been built close to the river from at least the early Bronze Age (c. 2000- 1600 BC).

■ Limited excavation at Eardisland appear to confirm that the deposition of individual high status artefacts into waterlogged or wet areas was a recurring activity in the middle Bronze Age (c. 1600- 1400 BC).

■ Prehistoric sites were under active erosion by the river soon after their construction and abandonment.

Chapter 4

Later prehistory from the project fieldwork

4.1   Upper Headlands, The Grove, Staunton-on-Arrow and the early Iron Age

Although the full extent of the Beaker period feature and potential settlement is not fully understood it would appear that site at The Grove continued to be a focal point on the floor of the river valley for a further 2000 years. The cropmark that was the original focus of the site investigation revealed interesting new information about rural enclosures dating to the late prehistoric period within the county. This then provides the focus for the present section of this report.

As explained in the previous chapter the excavations of the cropmark site at The Grove proved that the two concentric ditches seen in the aerial photographs dated to later prehistory. This was based upon two observations. Firstly, the outer ditch cut through what we now know to be a 'Beaker' period feature, so the outer ditch circuit must be at least later than the early Bronze Age (Figure 20). Secondly, during the excavation, fragments of Romano- British pottery were recovered from the uppermost fills of both ditches.

The outer ditch was a broad and deep ditch. The up-cast from the ditches would have produced a substantial bank. There was an indication that the up-cast bank material formed the initial backfill of the ditch. This appears to have happened fairly quickly, whereas the upper ditch deposits represent a more gradual silting up of the ditch. The entire assemblage of pottery (five fragments of Severn Valley ware and a small piece of Samian), were recovered from the uppermost deposit in the ditch. No other artefacts were found in the lower gravel deposits deeper into the ditch.

The inner ditch is narrower in width and shallower in depth but with steeper sides in comparison with the outer ditch. This inner ditch contained Romano-British pottery in its uppermost fill similar to those sherds retrieved from the outer ditch (*Appendix 3*).

The abraded nature of the pottery and its location in the upper most part of the backfill of the ditch may suggest that, like the Top Hales site, this pottery may not reflect the existence of Romano-British activity on the site itself but in close proximity to the site. The pottery may possibly have been deposited during a flooding episode of the near river channel. It may imply that even if the site had been abandoned it remained as a substantial earthwork within the landscape. This would seem to suggest that the site was in existence before the time of the Roman invasion of Britain. But what was its purpose?

Situated on the valley floor the double circuit of ditches seems to enclose a small gravel promontory that was bordered by a river channel or certainly by areas that were extremely marshy. As its location

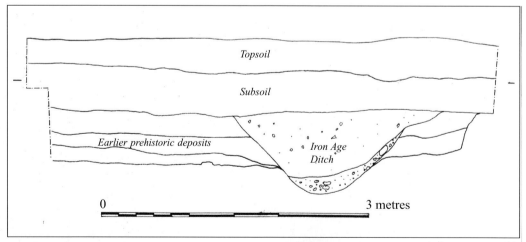

Figure 20 Section profile along eastern edge of Trench 2 showing the outer enclosure ditch cutting earlier prehistoric deposits.

Figure 21 Rowe Ditch looking southwards from Milton Cross. ©WNFC/MASH 99-C-0260

is overlooked on all sides by higher ground, it appears not to be very defensible as a fortification. It would appear too elaborate for farming management such as for herding stock, considering the investment that must have been required to excavate the ditches.

Perhaps the proximity of the site to water provides a clue to its purpose. Interest in rivers, lakes and wet places continued from the middle Bronze Age into the Iron Age as appropriate locations for ritual and perhaps this also meant that they had spiritual significance for people (Darvill, 1992). Perhaps this site is more comparable therefore with the dirk burial site of the Middle Bronze Age at Eardisland than we might initially assume. The ditches seem to define an inner and outer area that may relate to control of access. Could these ditches even have defined a 'mortuary' area, into which the priestly class wished to restrict access? This relates closely to the notion that a high proportion of bodies of the dead in the Iron Age were not interred in the ground, but were placed in rivers. This excavation has

provided a small insight into how the landscape might have been organised and regarded by the inhabitants of the Arrow Valley thousands of years ago.

Significance

The size of the enclosure at The Grove is on a scale that is often associated with the more visible historical monuments of the Iron Age such as hillforts within the county. What is not clear is the relationship of this lowland enclosure to the nearby Wapley Hill Iron Age hillfort. If the site is indeed an enclosure created to facilitate mortuary rites of this period, it is a remarkable find indeed.

4.2 Ox Pasture, The Leen Farm, Pembridge (LEE 03): the late Iron Age

Reasons for investigations

Across the Arrow Valley between the villages of Pembridge and Staunton-on-Arrow is the monument known as Rowe Ditch. The scale of this linear monument in the landscape can only really be fully appreciated from the air (Figure 21). What has also become obvious from aerial photography along and around the area of Rowe Ditch is the abundance of archaeological sites within this part of the Arrow Valley. These sites include the ring ditches at Top Hales (see Section 3.3).

To the north of the Top Hales site and to the eastern side of Rowe Ditch aerial photography from the 1970s onwards has recorded the location of a large rectangular ditched enclosure (Figure 22). What is significant about this site is that the southwest corner is overlain by Rowe Ditch and therefore predates its construction. The rectangular enclosure appears to be connected by a series of smaller ditches to a large circular ditch on the western side of Rowe Ditch. The arrangement of these cropmarks suggests multiple phases of activity on the site. The circular cropmark of a presumed Neolithic henge represents the earliest phase of activity that was subsequently incorporated into a later prehistoric settlement.

Rowe Ditch has been the focus of archaeological investigations in the past (Hill and Worthington, 2003) but these investigations have not provided a

Figure 22 Aerial photograph of the enclosures overlain by Rowe Ditch. ©CPAT 94-C-1171

conclusive date for the construction of the monument. It has been assumed that it dates to the post- Roman period or the Dark Ages (from AD 410 onwards). However we do know that it existed by the time of the AD 958 Anglo Saxon charter for the Staunton-on-Arrow estate (Lewis, nd). The aim of the excavation was to investigate the cropmark that is located below Rowe Ditch, which would hopefully enable the determination of a relative date for its construction.

The site investigations

The field which is currently under grass provided an opportunity to investigate the site early in the year and we are grateful to Tony Norman for permitting access to the site. During May 2003 two trenches were located at different points along the circuit of the rectangular enclosure ditch. The trenches were positioned by measuring off Rowe Ditch and comparing the distances to available aerial photography. The trenches, both ten metres in length, were located on different sides of the enclosure to assess any difference in the profile of the enclosure ditch and to increase the probability of retrieving datable artefacts (Figure 23). The trenches were also located to determine whether any internal features could be detected within the enclosure behind what is presumed to have been the bank created by the quarried gravel material. A mechanical digger was used to excavate the trenches

through the ploughsoil to the underlying gravel that was 0. 3 metres below the ground surface. The silt deposits of the ditch could easily be distinguished from the surrounding glacial gravels.

Results and site interpretation: A late prehistoric farmstead

No archaeological features were detected in the interior of the enclosure within the limited excavation trenches. The ditch sections in both of the trenches were excavated completely to reveal a wide and deep external ditch. The ditch was over 1. 2 metres deep from the ground surface and over 3 metres wide (Figure 24). The lowest deposits in the excavated segments of the ditch consisted mainly of gravel and represent the refilling of the ditch. This filling was with quarried material that must have been used as a bank that would have defined the site in the landscape. Above the initial gravel deposits was a silty layer that contained pottery.

From this fill of the ditch handmade mudstone tempered Iron Age pottery, likely to have been produced in the Martley area, was discovered. Nearly 40% of the pottery recovered from the site was this particular type of pottery fabric. One sherd formed part of an everted rim of a jar, which is known from other excavations to be a typically Late Iron Age vessel (see *Appendix 3*). Apart from this

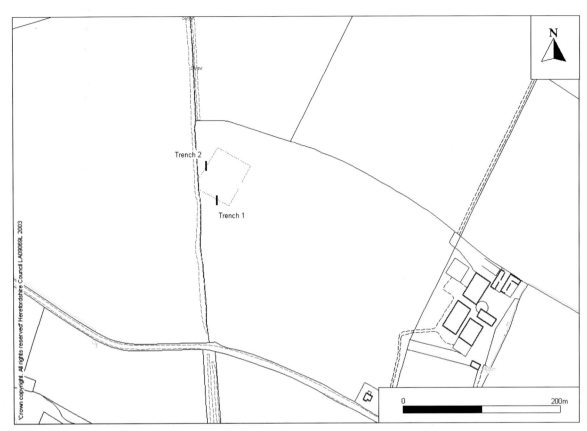

Figure 23 Location of the trenches at Ox Pasture, The Leen

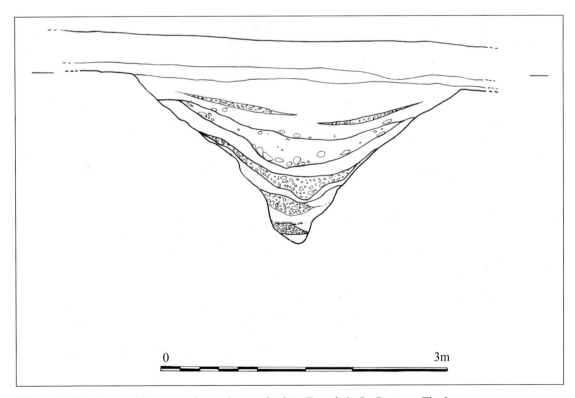

Figure 24 Section profile across the enclosure ditch in Trench 1, Ox Pasture, The Leen.

type of pottery further handmade pottery, known as Malvernian was also recovered. Both types of pottery fabric and form of the vessel suggests a late Iron Age date to when the enclosure was occupied. Both types of pottery have been found together on other Iron Age sites in the county, the most well known within the county being the excavations undertaken by Stan Stanford at Croft Ambrey hillfort (Stanford, 1974).

Above the Iron Age pottery within the upper most part of the ditch fills were sherds from later pottery types dating broadly to the Romano- British period. These included a Severn Valley ware cooking pot and a small fragment of Black Burnished Ware from Dorest that probably dates from after AD 120 (see *Appendix 3*). The Romano- British pottery was more abraded then that the earlier (Iron Age) pottery. It would appear that the occupants of this site were using native Iron Age pottery and fragments of later Romano- British pottery was deposited into the enclosure ditches as they gradually silted up as the site was abandoned. It is therefore suggested that this rectangular ditched enclosure is a small Late Iron Age/ Romano- British farmstead.

Significance

Although the scale of archaeological intervention was limited the excavation nevertheless revealed that the site was in existence at the turn of the millennium 2000 years ago and was constructed sometime between 100 BC and AD 100. By the time of the deposition of the Romano British pottery the enclosure ditch was already filling back up with up-cast material from the ditch. It may be possible to speculate that by the time of the mid second century the site had infact been abandoned.

However the greatest significance of this site was that it has provided for the first time a secure time-frame into which the construction of Rowe Ditch must fit. The pottery from this excavation appears to confirm the belief that Rowe Ditch cannot date to earlier than the Roman period and probably is a post- Roman monument. This is discussed further in the next chapter (see section 5.2).

Chapter summary: some key points

- The double-ditched enclosure at The Grove is so far a unique type of site not only within Herefordshire, but apparently in the wider Welsh Marches and West Midlands region.

- If, as seems likely, the ditches demarcated a 'sacred area' and activities in this area were associated with the placing of funerary deposits in the river, it is a discovery with wide implications and great importance nationally.

- The evidence from the later Iron Age at Ox Pasture, Leen Farm, confirms a trend emerging across the county, of sub-rectangular farmsteads being founded around 200- 100 BC and continuing into the Romano- British period.

Chapter 5

The Romano- British period and after

5.1 Middle Field, The Leen Farm (LMF 03); early farmsteads, fields and beyond

Reason for investigation

Analysis of the modern mapped field pattern during the Historic Landscape Characterisation project revealed that Rowe Ditch cut across the orientation of the modern field boundaries (Figure 25). It was speculated that perhaps this field pattern predated Rowe Ditch and the scale and orientation of the field pattern had been inherited and only slightly modified over the centuries (Ray and White, 2004). This idea was further supported by an aerial photograph taken in 1999 of what appear to be internal divisions detected as faint cropmarks within the larger modern day fields that now characterise the landscape in this part of the Arrow Valley. A series of varying sized enclosures could be observed orientated on a northwest- southeast axis and these appear to have been overlaid by other cropmarks on a different alignment. The clearest of these later cropmarks were the remains of Bagley Lane, a post-medieval routeway that passed through this field from Shobdon to Court of Noke.

The aim of the investigation was to establish the date of these cropmark boundaries, the general orientation of which appears to survive more widley within the current landscape as reflected by the modern field boundaries.

The site investigations

The lines of the most obvious cropmarks within Middle Field were rapidly transcribed by the author onto a map from the aerial photograph (Figure 26). Even without all the cropmarks recorded it was clear that there was a complexity of ditches which intersected each other in the middle of the field. As this potentially early field system covered a large area, two areas were targeted for 'key-hole' investigation. The field was under pasture and there was no indication on the ground of any of the buried archaeology. The trenches were therefore measured

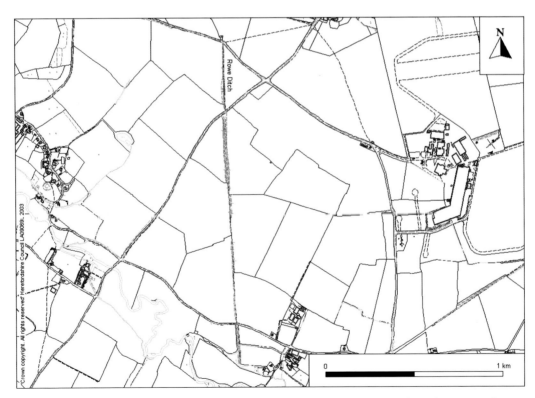

Figure 25 Rowe Ditch orientated north- south spans a landscape orientated northwest- southeast

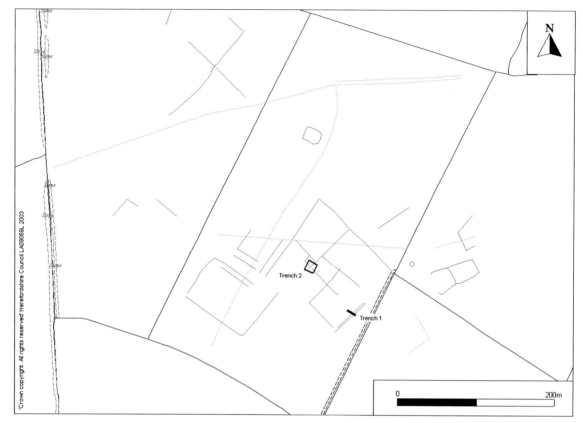

Trench 2

Trench 1

0   200m

Figure 26   Location of cropmarks and trenches within Middle Field, The Leen, Pembridge

off from the field boundaries. The first trench, 12 metres in length, targeted parallel double ditches on the easternmost side of the mapped cropmarks within the field. It was believed that these ditches were evidence for a possible droveway or track between the field enclosures. A 15 metre square trench was then excavated to understand the sequence of ditches near the centre of the observed complex of enclosures (Figure 26).

Results and site interpretation: Roman farming and trading

The first trench opened was located across the parallel NE- SW aligned ditches (not illustrated here). Romano-British pottery was recovered from these ditches. Both ditches were relatively shallow in comparison to the larger enclosure and ring ditches that had been encountered on the other sites investigated within the Arrow Valley. However there was another distinction. These ditches were full of pottery dating to the Roman period. Over thirty sherds of pottery came from a single ditch for example (see *Appendix 3*). The assemblage consisted of Black Burnished bowls from the late

second to mid third century, jars dating to the second century and Severn Valley ware tankards and mortaria also dating to the second to third century. Fragments of Samian pottery, imported from the continent, were also discovered. This pottery of high status implies that this feature is perhaps not a droveway as suggested as a possibility before the excavation. The double ditches appear to comprise one side of a large enclosure dating to the first or second century AD and similar to a site currently being investigated by Peter Guest of Cardiff University at Cold Furrow near Lyonshall village.

In the second trench Romano- British pottery was recovered from the five slots excavated across the NE- SW aligned ditch (Figure 27). The pottery included Samian ware imported from the continent, rimmed jars, Black Burnished table wares of the late second to mid third centuries and fragments of a Severn Valley ware tankard also dating from this period. As with the ditches in the first trench the pottery was recorded from the upper part of the ditch fills implying that there had been significant refilling or re-silting of the ditches before the disposal of pottery within them.

Once the ditch had silted up a large pit was cut into the line of the ditch (Figures 27). This was intecepted at the northern edge of the trench. The pit appears to have contained debris and refuse from small- scale industrial working. The section through the pit showed that it contained a series of charcoal dumps mixed with bands of clay possibly linked to small-scale industrial activity nearby. Pottery from this pit also included high status Romano- British fabrics that included a Black Burnished ware rimmed bowl dating to after AD 270. Molten glass was also recovered from the pit and at the very bottom of the pit iron hob- nails diagnostic of Roman shoes were recovered.

A later ditch cut across the top of the ditch filled with Romano- British pottery (Figure 27 and 28). The shallow nature of the ditch suggests it has been cut through the ploughsoil, although no cut could be distinguished on the edge of the trench. Running on a roughly east- west alignment it is believed to represent the remains of an old leat dating to the medieval or more likely the post medieval period.

This assemblage of artefacts suggests that we were not looking at a field system but a cluster of small enclosures near to a high status Romano- British farmstead or perhaps a small village surrounded by its field system in the wider landscape. Similar sites have been observed also by aerial photography on Salisbury Plain within the Training Area of the British Army (McOmish, Field and Brown, 2002). On Salisbury Plain some of the villages covered large areas and survive, in part, as earthworks. The remains of the village on Charlton Down extends over 25 hectares and is articulated by a series of tracks servicing well defined, presumably domestic, compounds. The range of artefacts retrieved from

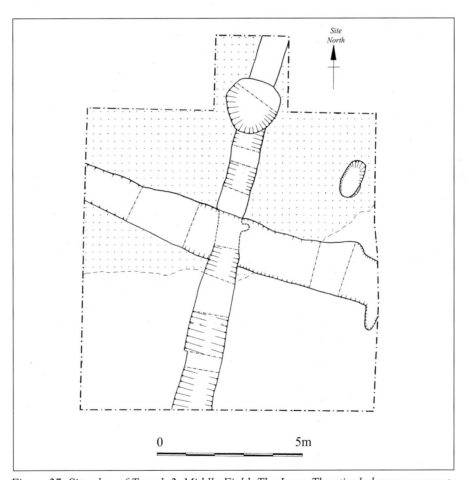

Figure 27 Site plan of Trench 2, Middle Field, The Leen. The stippled area represents the gravel subsurface and the blank area represents a clay subsurface or ditch/ feature fills

Figure 28 Photo of Trench 2, Middle Field showing the Romano-British ditch and pit under excavation

Charlton Down points to established agricultural communities (*ibid*). The layout and plan of this village site is remarkably similar to the plan of the cropmarks observed within Middle Field at The Leen (Figure 25). Although the concentration of cropmark enclosures at The Leen covers only 7 hectares, it is clear from the aerial photography that further cropmarks can be observed extending into the surrounding fields. The system as a whole may cover an area of over 20 hectares in extent.

All the pottery from the Middle Field site seems to date to after that of the pottery found on the rectangular farmstead cut by Rowe Ditch at Ox Pasture and this may indicate a settlement shift during the first centuries AD.

All of this suggests that people on this site nearly 2000 years ago were adopting aspects of the tastes and fashions of the invading Romans and from the high status pottery, were doing very well in trading with them. But what could they be trading? The most obvious commodity would perhaps be agricultural produce. The cropmarks seen on the aerial photograph within Middle Field may represent a large-scale reorganisation of landscape enclosure and settlement as a result of agricultural intensification. This view may be supported by the results of the work undertaken by the geomorphology team from Aberystwyth University on the chemical composition of the soils retrieved from samples cored from the Arrow's confluence to the south of Leominster (see Chapter 6 for details). It would appear that there is an increase in sediment derived from the lower reaches of the Arrow Valley during and after the Roman period. This may indicate changes in landuse including deforestation linked to agricultural intensification, changes in farming practices or re-organisation of the landscape through construction of new field boundaries or land drainage.

Significance

The abundance of pottery suggests that a sizable farmstead or broader settlement was located at this site and existed at the time of the Roman Conquest. This agrarian settlement was trading and profiting from the development of the market economy within Herefordshire and its abandonment may relate to the collapse of this system within this part of the empire. The Romano- British settlement could perhaps be seen as a predecessor to the villages that now exist within the Arrow Valley at Pembridge, Staunton and Eardisland.

It also suggests that perhaps the orientation of the field pattern today is derived from the organisation of the landscape nearly 2000 years ago. The orientation of the cropmark enclosures and the surrounding linear boundaries observed in the aerial photographs possibly suggest a continuity of the enclosure of the landscape through to the modern day.

However, the greatest significance resides in the apparent link between agricultural intensification and the rapid deposition of silts. It seems possible that a greater emphasis on arable production and drainage may have significantly accelerated run-off and erosion in these fields. This was perhaps an unsustainable change in farming practice, and could have had sereve consequences with the onset of climatically wetter conditions during the fifth century AD.

5.2 Rowe Ditch and the English settlement

Rowe Ditch remains as the most obvious feature of the early Anglo Saxon period within this part of the county. Its orientation and form suggest a defensive structure but apparent straightness of the sections of the Ditch suggest that it was planned with some knowledge of Roman survey techniques. The ditch now runs as an earthwork for nearly two miles but at one time extended further. It survives as an earthwork between the crossroad at Milton Cross southwards to Byletts on the Pembridge- Kington road. Aerial photography shows the line of the monument continuing up the slope of the Arrow Valley and excavations have revealed that it terminated near Vallet Covert in Shobdon parish. It is speculated that it also continued to the area of Pitfield farm at its southern most extent. Its name, Rowe Ditch could have derived from the Anglo-Saxon root 'Rof' meaning 'strong' and is recorded in a document of 1219 as 'Rogedich' or 'Rough Dyke'. This would certainly be apt, since the massive continuous bank with a ditch up to 3m deep on its western side must have formed a formidable barrier to movement down the valley from the west.

During the 1970s and 1980s ten excavations were undertaken along the line of the monument and were directed by David Hill (Hill and Worthington, 2003). These excavations although limited in time and scale of area investigated showed that the ditch survives in good condition below ground in places to a depth of over 2 metres and 5 metres wide.

As a result of the 2003 excavations it seems that the Rowe Ditch probably dates from the earliest arrival of the English in numbers in the Arrow Valley, c. AD 650 and that it was built by the English. It spans the valley, cutting through earlier settlements and landscape boundaries (see above). As such it reflects the division in the political landscape between incoming English settlers and the native Britons to the West during the Dark Ages. What is noticeable is that there appears to be no strategic advantage to the siting of Rowe Ditch within the Arrow Valley. A possible reason is that it represented a line of occupation and any settlement that existed to its east became an 'inherited' feature within the occupied territory, for example the field system and settlement at Middle Field. Therefore Rowe Ditch marked out the territory to the east as being 'England', and the area to the west as being occupied by the British whom the English had the affrontery to call 'foreigners' ('Welsh') in their own land.

It is not until several centuries later that the next evidence for Anglo Saxon activity manifests itself again as the linear dyke system of Offa's Dyke (Fox, 1955; Zaluckyj, 2001; Hill and Worthington, 2003). Built during the 8th Century the line of the dyke can still be seen in the landscape running northwards from Holme Marsh, parallel to the village of Lyonshall across Curl Brook (Figure 29). On the northern side of Curl Brook the bank has subsequently been used to define the parkland landscape around Lynhales and the remains of parkland iron railings can be seen sticking out of the bank. It continues as a continuous line just to the south of the Nusery at Lyonshall and is not detected again until to the south of Eywood near Berry's Wood in Titley. As with Rowe Ditch it is believed to form a territorial marker. The question remains: why is it so fragmentary within Herefordshire? Fox postulated this was due to dense forest that covered the county in areas and it was so impenetrable that it was unnecessary to construct the dyke and in the southern part of the county the River Wye formed the boundary (Fox, 1955). More recently opinion has focused upon the political situation during the Anglo- Saxon kingdoms and the possible rivalries and alliances between kingships. Where allegiances existed between Offa and his contemporaries in Powys the construction of a boundary was unnecessary (Hill and Worthington, 2003).

Figure 29 Offa's Dyke, marked by the tree- lined hedge in the centre of the photo remains a visible boundary within the landscape.

©WNFC/ MASH 99-C-0732

From excavations across the line of the ditch it would appear that it was never re-cut or cleaned out, which would imply neglect after it was built, perhaps as soon as the passing of Offa in AD 793. What is more important is that it has become symbolic of the divide between England and Wales and is used to define identities on both sides of the boundary (Feryok, 2001).

Significance

Neither Rowe Ditch nor Offa's Dyke permanently marked the 'frontier' between the English and the Welsh, and the English settlement continued westwards for several centuries. This is reflected in the dominance of English derived place- names throughout the Arrow Valley and into what is now modern- day Wales. In fact, no hard and fast boundary existed, and this area was ambiguously both Welsh and English, up until the Acts of Union in the sixteenth century. Rowe Ditch probably only served as an active 'frontier-work' for the first few years of English settlement. This idea is reinforced by the apparent fact that the traditional pattern of

settlement (marked by the orientation of field boundaries) was soon reverted to, and persists into the present day. The comparison between the relationship between these dyke monuments and the field pattern is of interest. Where Rowe Ditch appears to cut across the field pattern, in contrast Offa's Dyke particularly to the west of Lyonshall appears to be slotted into the field pattern and adheres to this orientation (Figure 29). This perhaps supports the idea that Rowe Ditch was imposed upon the landscape while the purpose of Offa's Dyke was to consolidate the frontier between kingdoms of the Anglo- Saxon period.

5.3 Medieval settlement in the Arrow Valley

Although no medieval sites were excavated as part of this project the landscape survey undertaken by the archaeology team along with earlier studies can build a picture of how the settled landscape of the Arrow Valley would have looked during the medieval period.

The location and extent of medieval settlement would appear to be quite obvious with the timber framed buildings at Pembridge and with known castles at Huntington, Kington, Lyonshall, Staunton-on-Arrow and Eardisland as well as links to religious foundations at Monkland and Titley. Indeed the pattern of dispersed village settlements within Herefordshire and particularly the Arrow Valley appears to have medieval origins but work undertaken by Herefordshire Archaeology since 1998 and most recently as part of this project has however revealed a more complex picture of medieval settlement than first imagined. In 2001 an appraisal on the medieval towns in Herefordshire was undertaken (Ray, 2001).

This reviewed a series of studies as well as reports on the historic towns in Herefordshire that had been compiled by the then Hereford and Worcester County Archaeological Service during the mid-1990s. These studies formed part of a wider study known as the Central Marches Historic Towns Survey (Dalwood and Atkin, 1998). The aim of the survey was to identify and specify the urban archaeological resource and to make recommendations regarding its extent and future management.

From the medieval towns listed as part of the Historic Towns Survey only Kington has remained as an 'urban' centre within the Arrow Valley. Other towns remain as focal points yet greatly reduced, such as at Pembridge and Lyonshall, and places such as Huntington have become a small cluster of farm buildings. It becomes clear that some of these towns were short lived and possibly only lasted for a couple of generations. The rivalry between the medieval lords was intense and the success of a township depended upon the political strength of the lordship. Evidence for medieval townships can derive from different forms of historical evidence, such as documents recording the granting of a market or fair, or archaeological evidence. In contrast to the earlier periods of history, many medieval features survive in the landscape above ground as earthworks such as house platforms.

In Lyonshall, the settlement has moved southwards to the modern road junction away from the higher ground near the church and castle. Over two hectares of earthworks survive and extend over a kilometre in length from the southern part of the village northwards to the church (Figure 30). These earthworks of burgage plots, house platforms and a market area survive extremely well and although the village was not recognised as a medieval town during the 1990s study, the earthworks would suggest a substantial planned settlement existed here. There is still a lot we do not know about these 'urbanised' medieval settlements in the Arrow Valley. For example, while the large castle at Huntington is well known the actual location of the associated medieval town has still not been conclusively mapped.

There is more evidence for medieval settlement in the wider landscape. As already mentioned aerial photography has revealed extensive remains of settlements at places such as Lawtonbury and Stagsbatch. Evidence for more medieval settlement comes from earthworks recorded as part of the field survey carried out during this project. This involved walking along roadways and public rights of way and recording any observed features within the fields.

Figure 30 Aerial photograph of the earthwork remains of the shrunken medieval settlement at Lyonshall.
© *WNFC/MASH 99-MB-0021*

The earthwork remains of a waterlogged moat at The Hyde, Leominster is already documented in the county Sites and Monuments Record (HSM 2557). However the extent of the surrounding earthworks that included sunken trackways that interconnect house platforms around the principal moated site has not been noted until now (HSM 34816). These earthworks extend into the surrounding orchards and are preserved beneath the trees (Figure 31). The Hyde is now a large farm with substantial brick buildings but this example demonstrates that many of the farms located within the valley that occupy sites at one stage covered a far larger area.

At Marston, Pembridge, earthwork platforms were observed around the hamlet and around what is now Marston House a large ditch could be observed that appears to define a large platform area (HSM 34817). It is suggested here that this is the remnants of manorial enclosure and that this is linked to a broad level area that is interpreted as a fishpond (HSM 34818). Local oral tradition appears to support this theory. This level area is now used as a football pitch. Also within the parish of Pembridge earthwork house platforms were observed within the pasture fields opposite Weston House (HSM 30645). Around Ivington platforms can also be also observed specially near to Ivington Green and some of the buildings that survive show clear indications of an early construction (HSM 34819). The best

preserved earthworks in this area can be observed to the east of Ivington Court where trackways and building platforms can be seen next to the confluence of the Stretford Brook and the River Arrow (HSM 34820).

The final category of evidence for medieval occupation in the Arrow Valley comes from observing the field patterns in the wider landscape. Within the farmed landscape field boundaries inform us of medieval occupation and of farming in common arable fields or 'strip-fields' systems. Although the land is no longer farmed in such a way the shape of field boundaries tell us that these strip fields have been enclosed and incorporated into the structure of the landscape today. Long curving boundaries define the edge of former furlongs, while dog- legs in the boundaries indicate the staggered enclosure of strip fields into a large enclosure or close. Where strips were ploughed across slopes lynchets would be formed. These lynchets can be observed on the slopes of the Arrow Valley and appear as terraces or steps that can be seen crossing fields today. Some of the best examples of lynchets can be seen to the north of Titley around Green Lane Farm and on the slopes of the Curl and Sour Brooks to the south of Lyonshall. Meanwhile, the furlongs of the town fields of Pembridge are outlined by later hedges in the Manley area southwest of the village. What the

Figure 31 Evidence for a more extensive settlement survives as earthworks in orchards around The Hyde, Leominster. © WNFC/MASH 01-C-2016

field patterns of the Arrow Valley can tell us of landscape change is discussed further in the next chapter.

Significance

It is clear that there was a large population living in the Arrow Valley during the medieval period and the settlement pattern that we see today as dispersed may have been far more nucleated that has been appreciated in the past. It is only through recent fieldwork that this former population is being discovered in Herefordshire. The question that is raised, is what happened to these settlements? Although there is no one answer, the plagues and Black Death of the Middle Ages must have been a factor. The proximity and density of population would have caused a catastrophic impact when plague struck. This would have been an impact from which the Herefordshire population never really recovered and this would have produced the dispersed the pattern of settlement that we see today.

Chapter summary: some key points

- In the period AD 100-200 a farmstead was established at Middle Field while the Oxpasture farmstead continued in occupation.

- This Middle Field farmstead had a double-ditched enclosure, contained imported fine pottery and other luxury items from some distance away, and sat within a wider landscape of farmed fields.

- The field system was defined by ditches that were re-cut and re-orientated through the Romano-British period down to at least AD 350.

- Intensification of arable farming in this landscape appears to coincide with geomorphological evidence (gained during this project) for increased erosion, runoff and silt deposition in the River Arrow itself.

- This system was brought to an abrupt end with the English settlement, probably c. AD 600. Rowe Ditch is now dated broadly to this period, and represents a major cultural dislocation. Even though the farmstead itself at Oxpasture was long abandoned by AD 600, its surrounding fields probably were not. Their orientation was completely ignored by the construction of the ditch, which was sited for a wider strategic purpose in the landscape.

- There is abundant evidence for medieval farming in the landscape of the Arrow Valley. Besides the better known earthwork and stone castles, there are many settlements, and much evidence for farming in open strips and using ridge and furrow methods of drainage, particularly in lower reaches of the valley.

PART THREE

LANDSCAPE CHANGE

Chapter 6

Holocene river development and archaeological sites in the Arrow Valley

Mark G. Macklin, Eric Johnstone, Paul A. Brewer, Philip G. E. Gnych and Anna F. Jones

Introduction

This chapter outlines the development of the Arrow Valley over the last 11,500 years, since the end of the last ice age, and considers the influence that changing river dynamics and flooding regime have had on human settlement and archaeological site preservation. Prior to this study the alluvial archaeology of the Arrow Valley was relatively poorly understood but preliminary surveys, particularly through the use of aerial photography and topographic maps, showed that there was enormous potential. For example, a prehistoric enclosure at The Grove near Staunton-on- Arrow and a probable Bronze Age ring ditch at The Leen near Pembridge are both truncated by old river channels.

Although this indicates a close relationship between settlement patterns and the location of the River Arrow, no research had been undertaken on river channel change in the Arrow catchment during either the pre-historic or historical periods. Indeed, until the start of this project, the only valley floor site in the whole of Herefordshire where Holocene (the post-glacial epoch, dated as beginning about 11,500 calendar years ago) river development and alluviation were constrained by radiocarbon (^{14}C) dating was at Wellington in the lower Lugg (Dinn and Roseff, 1992).

But why do we need to study river dynamics to interpret the alluvial archaeological record of the Arrow Valley? First of all, river erosion has the potential to destroy archaeological sites and to displace artefacts. Knowing if disturbance has occurred at a site, and whether artefacts are in primary or secondary context, are very important because they determine the degree to which cultural inferences can be made from the distribution of archaeological sites in a riverine landscape. Rivers, through deposition of fine-grained sediment, can also bury and preserve archaeological sites, and even entire former landscapes, beneath protective covers of alluvium. Where such sites remain waterlogged artefacts and organic material can be exceptionally well preserved. However, by their very nature, these sites are difficult to locate and are usually found through chance by farmers and engineers when carrying out excavation on valley floors.

Furthermore, it should not be overlooked that river sediments themselves constitute a unique record of environmental change, not only by virtue of the organic material they commonly preserve but also because their chemical and physical properties often provide a 'fingerprint' of past human activity in a river basin. In this context the analysis of river sediments and landforms can give us environmental 'lessons from the past' recording the successes and failures of earlier farmers, which are particularly useful for catchment managers today at a time of rapidly changing climate.

The principal objectives of our study were threefold: first, to document and ^{14}C date phases of river erosion and alluviation over the last 11,500 years in the Arrow Valley and to establish their probable causes; second, to evaluate the nature of human-river environment interactions in pre-historic and historical times; third, to provide guidance for decision makers on the conservation and management of the alluvial archaeological resource in the Arrow catchment.

The geology and geomorphology of the Arrow Valley: study site selection and research programme

The pre-Quaternary geology (Figure 32) and legacy of Pleistocene glaciations in the Arrow catchment have set the boundary conditions for Holocene river processes in terms of sediment size and availability, alluvial valley floor width and gradient, and the degree of connectivity between hill slopes and river channels. In this respect, the Arrow catchment can be divided into three physiographic units, each of which is characterised by a distinct suite of Holocene river deposits and landforms. The upland headwaters of the River Arrow, west of Kington, lie above 150 m and are underlain predominately by Silurian mudstones. This is an area of high relief, with relatively steep gradient channels that flow across valley floors of variable width. Narrower 'pinch points', formed by small valley moraines or dead ice topography, alternate with wider and lower gradient alluvial reaches located both up and downstream of valley floor constrictions. East of Kington the piedmont reach of the Arrow cuts across the southwest-northeast trending Kington-Orleton section of the Herefordshire End Moraine and extends as far downstream as Staunton-on-Arrow

(Dwerryhouse and Miller, 1930). The morainic deposits are mainly red till with Old Red Sandstone and contain Silurian siltstone, gabbro and dolerite erratics. The valley floor of the River Arrow in this piedmont reach is relatively narrow with limited space for terrace development and preservation. Between Staunton-on-Arrow and its confluence with the River Lugg, immediately south of Leominster, the River Arrow meanders over the Lower Old Red Sandstone till and alluvium covered lowlands following the course of a Late Devensian outwash plain that was constructed at the front of the Kington- Orleton Moraine. The valley widens markedly in this lowland reach and the margin of the Holocene alluvial valley floor has a distinctive 'hourglass' configuration with narrower sections at Eardisland, Arrow Green and Monkland.

Two of the four major study sites, The Grove and The Leen (Figure 32), were selected on the basis of their archaeology but were also considered to be representative of the Arrow Valley piedmont and lowland reaches, respectively. The other two sites, Folly Farm and Ivingtonbury (Figure 32), were selected for their palaeoenvironmental potential as the Arrow in its lower reaches is similar in character

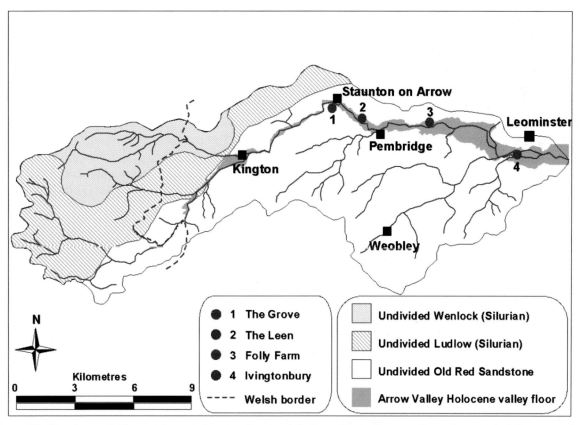

Figure 32 The Arrow Valley catchment showing the simplified pre-Quaternary geology, the extent of the mapped holocene valley floor and the four study sites

to river systems found in the eastern English Midlands (Brown and Keough, 1992) and at the fen edge in East Anglia (French *et al.*, 1992). In both these regions extensive buried palaeolandsurfaces and palaeochannels are found in conjunction with rich and well-preserved archaeology and palaeoenvironmental records. It was therefore anticipated that the Folly Farm and Ivingtonbury sites could be key areas for reconstructing human-river environment interactions in both the pre-historic and historical periods.

The geomorphological and palaeoenvironmental research programme was carried out in five stages:

1. Geomorphological mapping of the Holocene valley floor of the River Arrow from the Welsh border downstream to the River Lugg confluence – a total distance of 34 km (Figure 32). All river terraces and palaeochannels were identified by field walking and mapped onto OS 1:10,000 scale base maps. Colour vertical aerial photography was also used to map some palaeochannels which had poor morphological expression in the field but could be identified in the form of crop marks.

2. Sub-surface alluvial stratigraphy of river terraces and palaeochannels was established at the four study sites, 26 sediment cores (between 2-3 m in length) were collected using a hand-held percussion corer and 13 ground penetrating radar (GPR) transects (between 50-200 m in length) were surveyed.

3. Eleven samples of organic material (wood and plant remains) were extracted from the sediment cores for ^{14}C dating and pollen analysis; three from The Grove, two from The Leen, three from Folly Farm and three from Ivingtonbury. Radiometric dating of alluvial sediments in the Arrow Valley is critically important because it provides scientific rigour when trying to establish cause and effect relationships in human-river environment interactions.

4. To identify the probable sources of Holocene river sediment in the lower Arrow

Valley the geochemical composition of the sediment in each of the 10 cores was determined. Sediment samples were also taken from 30 sites in the headwaters and tributaries of the River Arrow to identify distinct geological source areas. The geochemistry of the core and source area samples was analysed using an inductively coupled plasma-mass spectrometer (ICP-MS) and was then compared using a multivariate mixing model to identify the relative sediment contributions of the distinct source areas to the main valley floor.

5. All geomorphological maps were converted to a geo-referenced digital format using ArcInfo and ArcView GIS software. A GIS is a database whereby features such as an archaeological site, an artefact or even the position of a river terrace or palaeochannel are assigned geographical co-ordinates and stored in a computer. A GIS is basically an 'electronic map' within which data of various kinds can be overlaid and compared. It has the enormous advantage that it can be easily updated and new types of data (provided they are geo-referenced) added.

Holocene river dynamics, environmental change and the Arrow Valley archaeological record

A sequence of four major Holocene terraces in the Arrow Valley has been identified from the geomorphological maps. West of Staunton-on-Arrow, in the upland and piedmont reaches of the catchment, these terraces are not continuous but are frequently truncated by younger fills. To the east of Staunton-on-Arrow, however, the four major terraces can be traced for significant distances downstream with Terraces 1 and 2, the uppermost terraces, being particularly prevalent. The geomorphological maps, used in conjunction with subsurface stratigraphical evidence and ^{14}C dating controls, have allowed a detailed interpretation of Holocene river dynamics, environmental change and the archaeological record to be made in the Arrow Valley, particularly at the four study sites where investigations were concentrated.

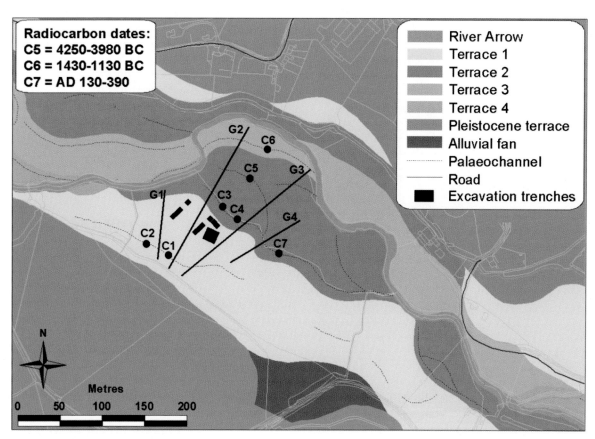

Radiocarbon dates:
C5 = 4250-3980 BC
C6 = 1430-1130 BC
C7 = AD 130-390

River Arrow
Terrace 1
Terrace 2
Terrace 3
Terrace 4
Pleistocene terrace
Alluvial fan
Palaeochannel
Road
Excavation trenches

N

Metres
0   50   100   150   200

Figure 33 Geomorphological map of The Grove study site showing core locations, GPR transects and archaeological trench postions

At The Grove near Staunton-on-Arrow (Figures 7 and 33) a Middle-Late Iron Age enclosure was sited on the uppermost terrace surface (Terrace 1) that appeared from aerial photographs to have been truncated by subsequent river activity. The archaeological excavation of the site also recovered Beaker pottery (2300-2050 BC) from Terrace 1 giving an initial minimum age for the unit. A radiocarbon date from a palaeochannel (C5 in Figure 33), however, indicates that Terrace 2 was the active floodplain of the River Arrow by 4250-3960 BC and that Terrace 1 had formed sometime prior to this. Further dating control from the palaeochannel on the lowest terrace at The Grove, Terrace 3, indicates that it was established by 1430-1130 BC. A third ^{14}C date, however, from palaeochannel core 7, suggests that Terrace 2 was reactivated in the Roman period at AD 130-390, probably during a phase of major flooding which is likely to have led to the northernmost edge of the Iron Age enclosure being truncated.

The second archaeological study site, at The Leen near Pembridge (Figures 13 and 34), featured a presumed Bronze Age ring ditch that sat adjacent

to a palaeochannel. The ring ditch located on Terrace 1 had been truncated by the palaeochannel meander on Terrace 2 indicating that this lower surface formed sometime after the Bronze Age. During the archaeological excavation, however, the recovery of Romano-British pottery from alluvial sediments infilling the ring ditch suggests that a more probable maximum age for Terrace 2 is AD 43-410. Core 5, taken from a palaeochannel on Terrace 3, was the only core at The Leen to yield organic material for ^{14}C dating; the dates returned (AD 890-1160, AD 770-990) indicate that the palaeochannel was active during Saxon times.

Further downstream in the Arrow Valley two more sites, selected for their palaeoenvironmental potential rather than their archaeology, were investigated. At Folly Farm near Eardisland (Figure 35) a palaeochannel on Terrace 2, which is inset against the Late Pleistocene terrace, yielded a date of AD 50-250 to give further evidence that this unit formed part of the active floodplain during Roman times. Dated samples from the palaeochannel at the neck of the meander on Terrace 3 (Figure 35,

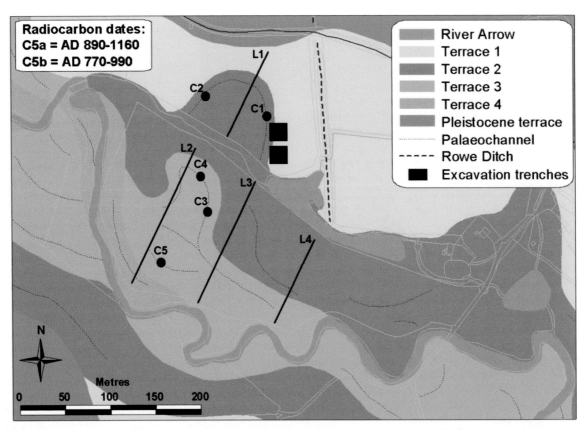

Figure 34 Geomorphological map of The Leen study site showing core locations, GPR transects and archaeological trench postions

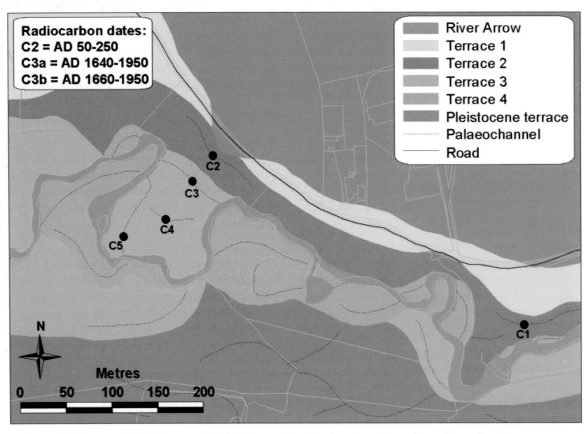

Figure 35 Geomorphological map of Folly Farm study site showing palaeochannel core location

Figure 36 Aerial photograph of the Ivingtonbury study site south of Leominster. ©WNFC/ MASH 00-MB-0280

C3) suggests that this channel was probably abandoned in the 17th or 18th century AD.

The final site was located at Ivingtonbury, south of Leominster (Figure 36 and 37), where relief across the wide valley floor is very subdued. Three cores were taken from palaeochannels on the surface of Terrace 2 which dated channel activity to the Late Iron Age (390-110 BC), the Roman period (AD 60-320) and Early Medieval times at cores 2, 1 and 3,

respectively. The varying ages of the palaeochannels indicate that this lowland section of the River Arrow has altered its course several times in the last 2,500 years, suggesting the presence of an anastamosing river system where channels can rapidly be abandoned and reactivated during flood events.

In Figure 38 ^{14}C dates (calibrated to calendar years and plotted at a 2-sigma range) of Holocene alluvial units in the Arrow and Lugg Valleys are plotted; dates from the Lugg Valley come from Dinn and Roseff (1992). Seven alluviation phases can be identified in the Arrow-Lugg system (Table 3) over the last 8,000 years or so, ranging in age from the Mesolithic up to the 17th century AD. Periods of accelerated sedimentation and river channel change in the Arrow Valley generally correspond with episodes of increased flooding found elsewhere in Great Britain as recently documented by Macklin and Lewin (2003, Figure 39). Certainly before the Roman occupation they also appear to coincide with cold and wet phases of climate (Figure 39). The age range for some phases of alluviation span several hundred years and further ^{14}C dates are

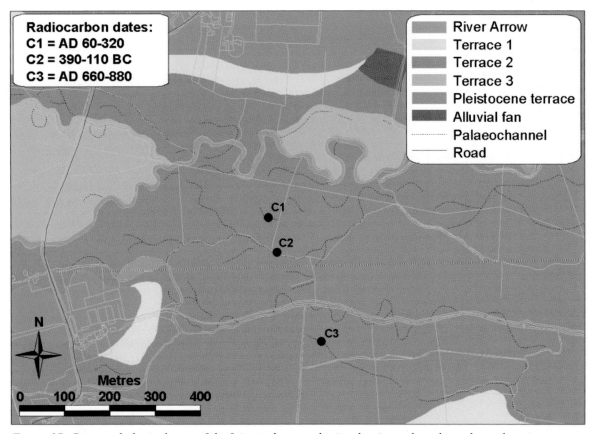

Figure 37 Geomorphological map of the Ivingtonbury study site showing palaeochannel core locations

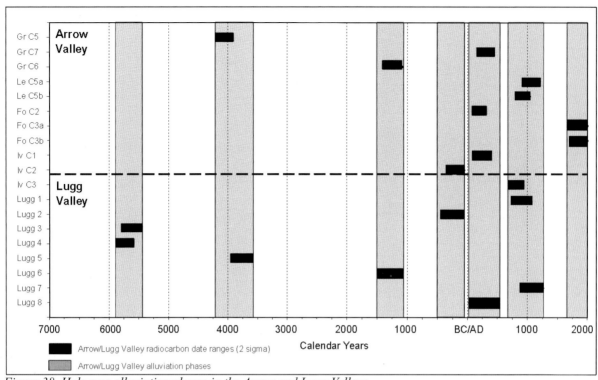

Figure 38 Holocene alluviation phases in the Arrow and Lugg Valleys

Alluviation Periods	Archaeological Period
5900 – 5500 BC	Mesolithic
4250 – 3640 BC	Neolithic
1510 – 1130 BC	Bronze Age
480 – 110 BC	Iron Age
AD 50-390	Roman
AD 660 – 1230	Middle Ages
AD 1660 - Present	Modern

Table 3 Holocene alluviation periods in the Arrow and Lugg Valleys with their corresponding archaeological periods

required to refine the Arrow Valley Holocene alluvial geochronology so the relationship between river development and specific climate events can be more thoroughly evaluated. Nevertheless, two phases of alluviation are particularly prominent in the Arrow and lower Lugg Valleys, which date to the Roman occupation (30 BC–AD 480) and the Middle Ages (AD 660–1280). These appear to have been significant particularly in terms of the geographical extent of alluviation with many parts of the Arrow Valley experiencing accelerated sedimentation during the Roman occupation and Middle Ages.

Geochemical analysis of a palaeochannel at Ivingtonbury, which was silting up during the Roman occupation, shows a major change in sources of sediment to the lower Arrow Valley shortly before and after AD 60-320 (Figure 40). Immediately prior to and during Roman times supply of sediment from the upland headwaters of the River Arrow (particularly the areas underlain by Silurian bedrock, Figure 32) declined. Coinciding with and immediately following the Roman occupation the proportion of river sediment derived from the Old Red Sandstone sources in the lower Arrow rose from around 25% to more than 50%. This marked increase in sediment supply from the lower relief areas of the Arrow Valley may be associated with changes in land-use including deforestation linked to agricultural intensification, changes in farming practices, re-organisation of the landscape through construction of new field boundaries or land drainage. It is interesting to note that in the upper 80 cm of the core the sediment contribution from upland (Silurian) sources slightly increases but not to values recorded before the Roman occupation. Alluvial sediments from another palaeochannel at Ivingtonbury, which date to the Middle Ages (AD 660-880), show that sediment sources by this time were slightly different with the contribution from the Old Red Sandstone areas of the lower Arrow falling to below 40% and

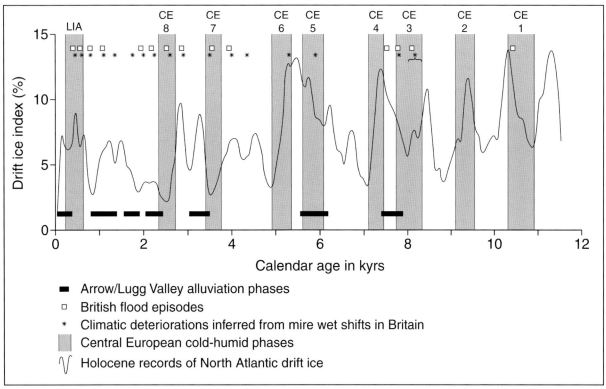

Figure 39 Comparison of Arrow/ Lugg alluviation phases with British Holocene flood episodes and proxy climate records for Britain, Central Europe and the North Atlantic

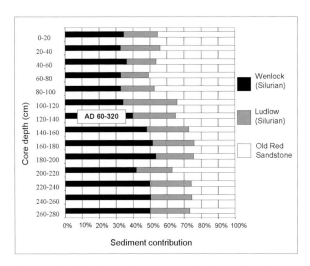

Figure 40 Relative sediment contributions from the major geological source areas in the Arrow Valley to Ivingtonbury Core 3 in the lower reaches of the catchment

the contribution from the Ludlow source areas of the uplands increasing to over 30%. This second core shows that minor fluctuations in contributions from the sediment source areas continued after the Early Medieval period but that the overall pattern of relative contribution remained stable.

The role of Geographical Information Systems in archaeological interpretation and management

A GIS has been constructed for the entire Arrow Valley floor from the Welsh border downstream to its confluence with the River Lugg at Leominster. This has been particularly useful as it has allowed, for the first time in Herefordshire, the systematic integration of archaeological and geomorphological datasets at the catchment-scale. To illustrate the potential of this approach the Sites and Monuments Record (SMR) has also been overlaid onto the valley floor geomorphological maps (Figures 41, 42 and 43).

A total of 37 archaeological sites and monuments are recorded on, or immediately adjacent to, the Holocene valley floor of the River Arrow. Only five of these are located on the narrow valley floor upstream of Staunton-on-Arrow (Figure 41) where poorer soils and fewer areas of refuge from flood events are likely to be partly responsible for lower rates of pre-historic and historical human activity. The number of archaeological records increases downstream of Staunton on Arrow (Figures 42 and 43) where the wider valley floor with larger expanses of more fertile alluvium creates a more

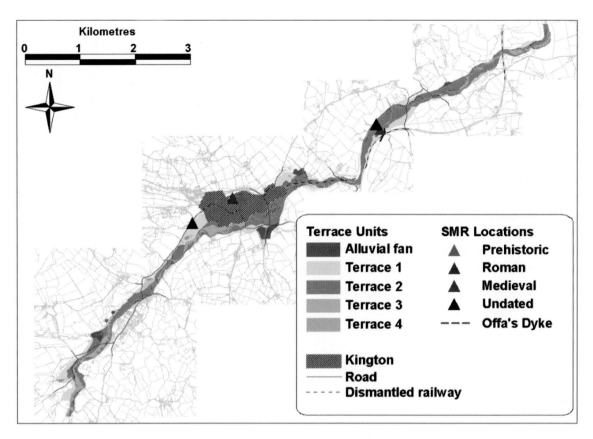

Figure 41 Geomorhological map of the Holocene valley floor of the Arrow Valley between the Welsh border and Staunton-on-Arrow with SMR locations overlaid

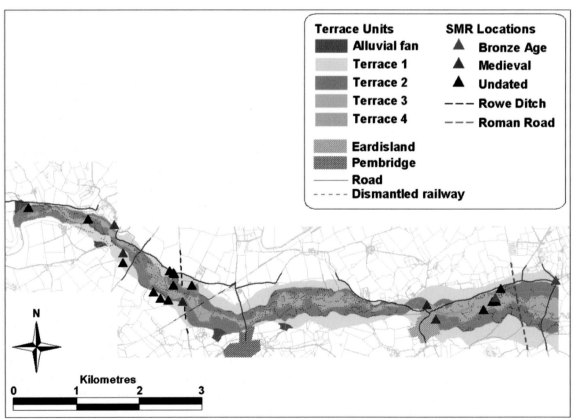

Figure 42 Geomorhological map of the Holocene valley floor of the Arrow Valley between Staunton-on-Arrow and Arrow Mill with SMR locations overlaid

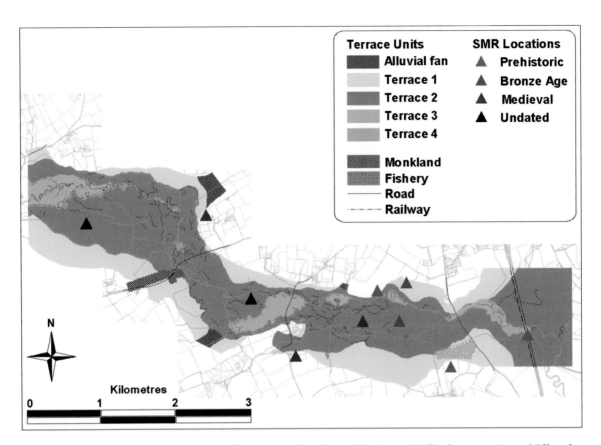

Figure 43 Geomorphological map of the Holocene valley floor of the Arrow Valley between Arrow Mill and Broadward with SMR locations overlaid

hospitable environment for human settlement and agriculture. A large majority of records are also located on the Holocene valley edge or on the uppermost terrace (Terrace 1) which would have provided easy access to the River Arrow whilst offering some protection from flood events.

Those SMR records that have been dated as Prehistoric or Bronze Age are generally located at the edge of the Holocene valley floor or on Terrace 1. Exceptions to this are two Prehistoric and Bronze Age records located on Terrace 2 south of Leominster (Figure 43). Both these records are finds and probably reflect artefacts that have been recovered in a secondary context following human displacement or fluvial reworking. Downstream of Eardisland, however, one more Bronze Age record that is thought to be a barrow cemetery is located on Terrace 3, which is considered to post-date the Bronze Age period. This presents an apparent anomaly between the archaeological and geomorphological records and identifies the site as a priority for future research. Records dating to the Roman and Medieval periods present no such chronological difficulties though as they are all located on the edge of the Holocene valley floor or on Terraces 1 and 2.

The application of GIS to alluvial archaeology in the Arrow Valley is a significant innovation by providing information on the mobility and/or survival of archaeological sites of various ages, and how these may have been influenced by Holocene river dynamics. Furthermore, the GIS-based approach provides a robust framework for interpreting, conserving and managing the alluvial archaeological resource as well as a research tool for identifying promising areas for future study.

Conclusions and future research

Geomorphological investigations have demonstrated the highly dynamic nature of the River Arrow in both pre-historic and historical times, with seven distinct phases of alluviation being identified in the last 8,000 years. Prior to the Roman occupation these alluviation periods appear to have been controlled primarily by variations in climate. The first large-scale impact of land use change on river sedimentation is marked during the Romano-

British period by accelerated rates of erosion in the middle and lower parts of the Arrow Valley. This research, which has also demonstrated the complementary nature of geomorphological and archaeological methods of investigation, makes the Arrow Valley one of the most thoroughly geomorphologically researched rivers of its size in western Britain.

A great deal of potential still exists, however, for future research in the Arrow Valley. For example, further coring of palaeochannels adjacent to archaeological sites, particularly at The Grove where Beaker pottery was recovered and downstream of Eardisland where the Bronze Age barrow cemetery is located, would enhance our understanding of human-river environment interactions in important areas of the River Arrow. Further coring at archaeological sites to collect organic sediments and peat samples for pollen analysis would also allow patterns of valley floor vegetation to be reconstructed and facilitate further ^{14}C dating to refine the Holocene alluvial geochronology. In the lower Arrow Valley, particularly south of Leominster, GPR surveys and targeted coring could be used to identify buried archaeological landscapes that may contain well-preserved waterlogged organic material. Finally, investigations into Medieval and Post-medieval water management practices in the lower reaches of the catchment would allow their impact on the more recent development of the River Arrow to be evaluated.

Acknowledgements
The authors would like to express their sincere thanks to all of the farmers and landowners in the Arrow Valley whose cooperation and assistance enabled this research to be undertaken.

Chapter summary: some key points (P. White)

- This study is the first such correlated geomorphological mapping and investigation parallel with archaeological site investigation in the Welsh Marches.

- The rationale and operation of a distinctive approach to the investigation of post-glacial river valley catchment development is set out in this chapter.

- Criteria for site selection for detailed study included the presence of archaeological sites close to developed fluvial landscapes, and selection of areas of the lower reaches of the river with significant palaeo- environmental potential.

- A series of palaeochannels were mapped, using ground penetrating radar and radiocarbon dated at The Grove, with a complex sequence of channel formation revealed and closely linked to the archaeological sequence.

- The extent of erosion due to dynamic river channel change was revealed at The Grove and the Top Hales site at The Leen. A phase of alluviation dated to the Romano- British period (AD 60-320) may suggest a date for this erosion.

- Survey at Folly Farm, Eardisland revealed that the course of the river channel remains active from the late medieval to modern day.

- Near to its confluence at Ivingtonbury the river has altered its course several times in the last 2,500 years, where abandoned channels appear to be reoccupied during flooding.

Chapter 7

The cultural landscape from maps and boundaries

7.1 Introduction

This chapter explores three different ways in which landscape change can be studied using maps and fieldwork. Each approach brings a different perspective to our understanding of landscape development through time and the implications of landscape change for the determination of what is inherited as landscape from generation to generation.

One approach is to compare changes in land-use between maps dating from different time- periods. The registering of change in land use can provide an indication of the level of impact that changes in land management had through time and may explain why what we see surviving in the landscape today, has endured in this way.

Another approach involves the cross-referencing of mapped features between maps. The presence or absence of features can help gauge the development of important historical elements in our landscape from settlements to roads. The third approach

1754	Isaac Taylor
1762	Em. Bowen
1789	John Carey
1801	John Cary
1832	Ordnance Survey
1835	Bryant
1839-1850	Tithe Apportionment
1852	British Gazetteer
1880s	1st edition Ordnance Survey
1902	Jakeman and Carver
1905	Ordnance Survey
1930s	British Land Utilisation
1964	Ordnance Survey
1980s	Ordnance Survey
1999	Ordnance Survey

Table 4 List of maps used during map analysis as part of the Arrow Valley project

achieves its interpretations not from historical maps but by analysing the field boundaries on today's maps and deducing their possible importance in creating the historic character of an area. This provides a narrative on the historical development of the landscape that may not be captured by earlier maps, since the earliest countywide maps take us back only to the 16th century. Many strong influences on landscape have earlier origins than this and are still manifest within the landscape.

For the landscape change study a total of 15 maps of different dates was used to assess the nature and scale of landscape change over the past three hundred years (Table 4). This meant that the mapping scale varied considerably between maps.

7.2 Change in land use from maps

Mapping horizons

In calibrating land-use change, it is helpful to review sources that cover the whole landscape. For this reason, individual estate plans, though enlightening for the study of small areas of the landscape, are less use for landscape-wide comparison.

What it is most useful to do, then, is to find 'benchmark' mapping that indicates what land was being used for what purpose, at a given time. The problem with seeking to do this is that Ordnance Survey maps concern themselves primarily with hard physical features, and especially boundaries. Although orchards are shown, it is often difficult to deduce (for instance) what land was being used as meadows, and what ground was cultivated.

For this study, therefore, a comparison was made between the Tithe Maps of the period 1839-50 that possessed a key to the land use by providing field names, and later mapping specifically designed to capture land-use. The Tithe Maps, then, provide the earliest horizon currently available. The best 'medial horizon' is provided by the Land Utilisation Survey of the 1930s. Finally, there is the 2003 horizon provided by the present survey of fields in the ten Arrow Valley parishes. Most usefully, these surveys are spaced about a century apart.

Tithe Maps

Dating towards the end of the first half of the 19th century, the Tithe Maps provide information on the rural landscape on a parish by parish basis. The transcription of these Tithe Maps by the Herefordshire Field Names Survey of the Woolhope Naturalists' Field Club has made this source of information very accessible. Not only do the maps record the size and shape of the fields but also the names and land-uses of each land parcel. In the Arrow Valley, Staunton-on-Arrow is the earliest Tithe Map recorded, dating from 1839. Meanwhile Leominster, the latest, dates to 1850. However, most maps date between 1840 and 1845. One of the downsides of studying the Tithe Maps is that it is very difficult to compare rapidly between maps of different periods over a large area.

One of the first observations of the landscape that can be made is the dominance in the 1840s of meadow and pasture along the course of the river Arrow and its tributaries. Further away from the river channel the land use changes to a mixed arable regime and a landscape that is perhaps not so removed from what we see today. Each parish contained areas of arable farming. The area to the west of Huntington village and to the east along the Kington road was dominated by arable fields, as was the area along Noke Lane, Pembridge. The interfluve between the Arrow and the Curl Brook is dominated by arable farming.

The large number of Hopyard fieldnames along the valley testifies to the existence of a kind of land use that is now limited to a small area at the eastern end of the Arrow Valley around Monkland and Ivington. It is likely also that this was an ephemeral presence, since the Herefordshire hop-growing industry only developed to any scale as late as the end of the 18th century

In Kington parish all of the slopes of Hergest Ridge were under arable cultivation with grassland located only on the lower parts of the valley floor. This ridge is now characterised by the dominance of grazing. This upland cultivation was not restricted to this part of the valley and continued along the southern slopes of Bradnor Hill and Wapley Hill.

One of the interesting trends in the arable landscape of the mid- 19th century was the retention of narrow strip fields that probably dated to the Medieval period, or (as enclosed land parcels) at least to the early Post-medieval period. These are most noticeable just to the west of Pembridge village, around Lewis Wych in Lyonshall, and around Eardisland at Lower Hardwick, Shirl Field and Riddimoor Field.

Land Utilisation Survey maps

Just before the Second World War a land utilisation survey was undertaken for the county by the Ministry of Works. The publication of the survey was delayed due to the outbreak of war but it was published in the post- war period as a document commenting on the reconstruction and restructuring of Britain after the war effort. The report included assessing areas for new building construction and the use of farmland was mapped based upon the pre-war survey. It is study of this map that provides a benchmark to changes in land use between the middle and end of the 20th century.

The map shows that the Arrow Valley within Herefordshire is dominated by grassland. In this respect, the general trends observed from the Tithe Maps of the mid-19th century continue through to the 1930s. The land next to the river channel is dominated by meadow, with small patches of arable cultivation on the higher ground of Hergest and Huntington. It would appear that the river provided a divide between farming regimes.

On the north side of the river Arrow pasture and meadow dominates the landscape from Titley to Eardisland. The area on the southern side of the valley is a mixed farming regime with arable and grassland in equal measure especially around Lyonshall and Broxwood. Across the landscape small areas of orchard were located near to the main farm buildings for the personal consumption of cider as opposed to commercial use. The analysis of change between the 1930s and today is discussed in Chapter 9 in more detail.

7.3 Earlier landscapes and settlement from maps

One aspect of the landscape study was the documentation of change through map regression

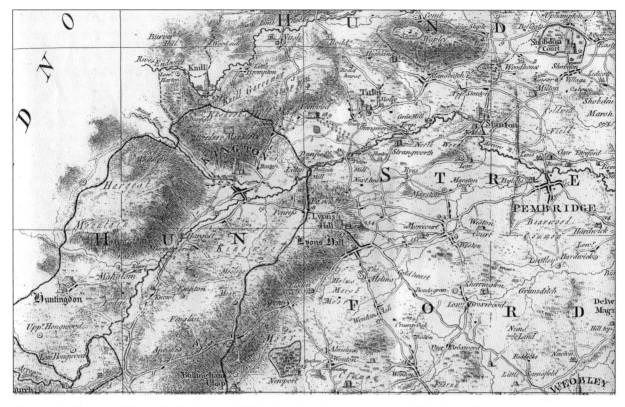

Figure 44 Extract of Isaac Taylor's map of 1754 showing the western part of the Arrow Valley

analysis. This study was not without its limitations. It became clear soon after the analysis had commenced that the quality of detail captured by the cartographers through the ages varied considerably. In particular the line of routeways varied considerably as did the representation of woodland and the size of settlements and villages within the study area.

However general trends to the changing landscape could be captured such as changes in the size of settlements, the location of mills and industry, woodland and parks, roads and routes along the valley, as well as recorded ancient historical sites.

Settlement and placenames

The study of old maps can provide an insight into how the landscape has changed. This can include changes in the settlement pattern with places becoming abandoned and reduced in size or new settlements being established, while place-names can give an indication of land use or as to how people saw the landscape.

In the upper reaches of the Arrow at Huntington, the earliest map of 1754 (Figure 44) records the settlements of Upper and Lower Hongwood along

with the settlement of Huntington. The name itself is derived from the Welsh *Hen-goed* meaning 'Old Wood' (Bannister, 1916). In 1789 Middle Hongwood appears for the first time on the maps and this seems to imply that there is a significant population in this part of the county which is now characterised by dispersed and isolated farms. By 1832 these settlements change to their existing place-names of Hengoed. This is interesting as part of the manor of Huntington was in the Welshry of the Marcher lordship of Kington and shows how the Welsh placename 'Hengoed' had been anglicised on the earlier maps. This does not necessarily mean the existence of large areas of woodland but perhaps reference to the wooded nature of the landscape with abundant farmland trees located in long establishes hedgerows and enclosures. Another interesting aspect is the small number of Welsh derived place-names in the Arrow Valley, which is perhaps not surprising, considering the proximity to the border. Places such as Penllan, Huntington and Penrhos, Lyonshall all suggest a name derived from Welsh. Further eastward along the valley the names are dominated by Old English.

Further down the valley the 1754 map appears to suggest a sizeable population or cluster of buildings at Dunfield (Downfield), Kington; Little Empton, near Chickward and The Lowe, Pembridge. This may suggest a settlement or large house that employed people to work the land have gradually over time become isolated farms.

Woodland and trees

The study of the extent of woodland and its changes between historical maps is of interest in the research into how the landscape has been managed. The loss of woodland may signal pressure to increase other land uses such as arable farming so to increase yields. The loss of woodland has wider implications that may relate to an increase in run-off, erosion on hill slopes for example. It was once thought that patches of woodland throughout Herefordshire reflected the clearance of a primeval woodland that nearly covered the entirety of the county (Rackham 1988; Fox, 1955). From recent fieldwork undertaken by *Herefordshire Archaeology* it has become clear that many of the woodlands so far surveyed have the remnants of earlier landscapes contained within their boundaries. Many of these historical features relate to arable farming and consist of ridge and furrow, lynchets and enclosure

boundaries that clearly demonstrate that woodland has not always been established in these areas of the landscape, and much of the present day woodland may date to the late- medieval and post-medieval period.

One of the problems in attempting to assess change in woodland was that it was soon realised after examining the early maps that it is not until Bryant's map of 1835 that the actual extent of woodland is marked on. However it was possible to compare the Ordnance Survey maps of the mid-19th Century with modern maps and characterise areas in terms of loss or gain in woodland to provide an appreciation of the extent of woodland cover.

There has been loss of woodland at Vallet's Wood near Cabal, Pembridge while vestiges of this woodland appears to survive in the corners of the fields. There has also been limited clearance of woodland around Penllan, Huntington and the woodland around Staunton Park has reduced in size. In the northwest corner of Pembridge parish Northwood Coppice, now called Grove Wood, did extend over Noke Lane between Northwood Farm

Figure 45 The woodland around Titley and Eywood Park with Lyonshall Park Wood in the background.
©HAAS 03-CN-0531

and The Forge. This area of tree clearance corresponds with an area of Parliamentary Enclosure Award (Oliver, 2003). The single most substantial change in tree cover within the Arrow valley occurred during the latter part of the 19th century with the clearance of Kingswood to the south of Kington.

But it has not just been woodland loss, there are areas of 'new' planting. In Lyonshall parish the woodland around Jack's Ditch Lane has experienced a change in namefrom Wyson's Coppice to Penrhos Wood and has also changed shape. Many of the woodland areas have moved but are very similar in size or slightly larger when compared to the 1835 Bryant map. Mowley Wood and Lyonshall Park Wood have both increased slightly in size and have altered in shape and this provides an indication of continued management of woodland.

Another aspect of studying woodland was that some woods have remained the same size but have been converted from broadleaf woodland into dense forestry plantations. An example of this is at Forest Wood, on the southern slope of the Gladestry brook to the southwest of Kington and Stocking Wood, northwest of Titley Court. Likewise Wapley Hill has undergone radical changes in its forestry. This has implications for the character of woodland managementand perhaps the survival of earlier features that might be contained within the woodland.

Beyond the recording of land- use changes from maps a field survey within woods can provide evidence for former activity before the planting of woodland. Often pre- woodland features survive along with evidence of industrial activity associated with woodland. The study and survey of woodland is important as archaeological features from early periods of history survive under later woodland, depending upon its management. During the time of this project two woodland surveys were undertaken by staff of Herefordshire Archaeology within the Arrow Valley at Molwey Wood and Wapley Hill (Lello, 2003; Williams, 2003). These two areas represent the largest woodlands within the area and the rapid walk- over survey was undertaken as part of a study designed to document the archaeology of woodland across Herefordshire.

Mowley Wood is located on the north side of the River Arrow, approximately 2km west of Staunton-on-Arrow. On its southern and eastern sides, the wood is bordered by the river, and to the west, by the course of a disused railway line. On the north side, fields border the wood. The woodland sits on a plateau above the river. The steep south and east facing slopes, and the north- eastern areas, are covered by deciduous woodland. Immature deciduous woodland covers a narrow strip on the north- western edge and conifer plantations cover the western and central areas. Much of the central plateau area within the woodland has been cleared.

The most common archaeological features identified related to the medieval and post- medieval period consisting of quarries. Sandstone has been quarried from the underlying bedrock of the Lower Old Red Sandstone formations presumably for building purposes. Woodland management features are also present, primarily in the form of holloways and trackways, and woodland compartment boundaries. The area of Mowley Wood is criss-crossed with holloways and trackways and a holloway gave access from the south to an area of shallow quarry scoops.

A number of woodland boundaries were recorded in the form of banks and ditches. Several of these features provide evidence of changes in woodland boundaries. Within the area one saw- pit was recorded. Also within the present woodland, are the remains of a single storey stone-built cottage with a surrounding garden. From the configuration of the various banks in the northern area of wood it is postulated that these represent former farmed enclosures which have now been absorbed into the woodland. Four upright stones were recorded; they may have functioned as boundary markers. Also in the northern area of the wood, a sub circular platform was recorded near a large oval pond with ornamental plants surrounding it. The Ordnance Survey 1st edition maps of the 1880s records an enclosure at this location, described on the Staunton-on-Arrow Parish tithe map of 1839 as a cottage and garden (Lello, 2003).

At Wapley Hill, the management is clearly different with commercial forestry plantation covering most of the hilltop and slopes. Historical features and structures were also recorded within the woods of The Warren, Crabtree Wood and Goden's Wood that forms part of the Wapley Hill Woodland Management area. These date from the Iron Age and the medieval periods, but the majority illustrate the management of the woodland resource in the Post- medieval period, for example saw pits, charcoal burning platforms, quarries and woodland management boundaries.

The significant exception to this was identified within The Warren, an area almost totally lacking evidence for woodland management. The most significant boundary identified, consists of two phases and surrounds the whole of the area known as the Warren. The first phase consists of an earth bank onto which a stone wall was later constructed. While the date of the earlier bank is unclear, it is known that the wall was constructed in 1725. This survey has also shown that the area now covered by The Warren was not wooded in the 18th and 19th century. Although a number of field boundaries were identified that date to this period they are few in number, encompass large areas and most likely represent an area that was used as common or communal pasture. To the south of the existing Stansbatch to Byton road, in Crabtree and Goden's Woods, there was an abundance of woodland management features, and the remains of a possible medieval field system (Williams, 2003).

What these surveys demonstrate is that the remains of former land use and land management is stored within the woodlands of Herefordshire and it is only now that we are beginning to fulfil the potential of woodland archaeology to elucidate that history

Parks

When we think of parks today we often think of grand designs and the elaborate planting of exotic species of plants and trees. This is only half- true as these types of park were often created from the middle of the 18th century onwards on former farmland or within areas of earlier parkland, where the purpose of the park was far from ornamental but to provide an area for hunting. The recent publication by the Herefordshire and Worcestershire Gardens Trust of the history and condition of parks in gardens in the county provides a basis for further research (Whitehead, 2001). The Garden Trust used the first edition Ordnance Survey maps of the late

19th century as their primary historical point of reference (*ibid*). By undertaking a rapid review of this publication and cross referencing areas of parkland to the maps that predate the Ordnance Survey it is possible to build a picture of the development, continuation and abandonment of parkland within the Arrow Valley.

The earliest forms of park were derived from the feudal ownership of land and linked to hunting in deer parks and the control of warrens. In today's landscape there are areas of specifically designed parks and extensive gardens throughout the Arrow Valley for example at Eywood Park, Titley Park, Staunton Park, Moor Court and Broxwood Court. However the review of the county scale maps revealed the limited nature to which the existence of parkland was recorded. There were however indicators for these planned landscapes based upon place-names such as at Lyonshall Park, and on Taylor's 1754 map the tree avenue at Eywood is recorded. It is also interesting to note that this avenue represents the only trees to be recorded by Taylor as a feature within the entire Arrow Valley and suggests that the parkland was already becoming established.

Therefore it can be seen that the parks can be divided into two categories. One set of parks are derived from medieval formation while the other group established was during the post- medieval period as part of the increased interest in the picturesque movement and garden and park landscaping. The possibility of parks with medieval origins are documented along the Arrow Valley.

For instance, a park at Huntington is first mentioned in 1265 and there would have been a park situated around Hergest Court at the same time. A deer park is documented at Lyonshall and survives as a placename within the parish. This deer park would undoubtedly have been linked to the de Lacy castle constructed at the northern end of the village, probably some time at the end of 11th century and the beginning of 12th century. Not all deer parks are this old. Staunton Park, for instance, was designed in the mid- 19th century while the park around Titley Court was probably not formalised until the late 18th century. It has also been speculated there may be a medieval origin to the parkland around Burton Court near Eardisland, although further investigation is required (*ibid*).

Although the use of water in the wider landscape such as in water meadows has not been recorded on the early maps, the scale of industry is acknowledged and mills are recorded. During 1970 a survey was undertaken of the mills on the River Arrow and its tributaries by the Archaeology section of the Woolhope Naturalist Club (Pye, 1970). In total 37 mills were recorded. There has been a long tradition of milling upon the Arrow as a mill is mentioned in the Anglo- Saxon Estate Charter for the Staunton Estate in 958. It has been postulated by Beryl Lewis that this mill is in the location near to Court of Noke, although no conclusive evidence has been found on the ground yet (Lewis, nd).

In the present project, the study of the 1754 map revealed eighteen mills along the course of the Arrow. Mills on the Herefordshire stretch of the Arrow start at Elcox's Mill (now Park Style mill) on the parish boundary between Huntington and Kington and continue to the mill at Ivington. However the greatest concentration of mills are between Kington and Staunton where twelve mills are recorded over a distance of just over six miles (Figure 46). Most of these survive as buildings if not as working mills, as the house name now provides an indicator of its former use. A mill is recorded at Hunton Bridge, Titley up until 1801 map but does not appear on any of the later maps. The importance of milling and the level of rural industry in the Arrow Valley is reflected firstly in the number of mills recorded and secondly by the presence of mills with two waterwheels, at Staunton-on-Arrow and Hergest.

It is not until the 1830s that the full extent of mills and the associated leats and mill- races are mapped and recorded comprehensively by the Ordnance Survey and the location of weirs and sluices are not mapped until 1880s. It is from this mapping epoch that the extent of water management can be appreciated. Mill races, used to take water off the river channel to power the water wheels could extend over a considerable distances, for example at Eardisland over half a mile. Apart from milling the Arrow was also the site of metalworking with a forge at Strangeworth on the boundary between Titley and Pembridge. A forge is mentioned in a document of 1695 and was again noted in 1717 but appears to have ceased working by 1736 (HSM 370). It has been recently suggested that it was not a forge as such but a bloomery to extract iron from the ore. It was replaced by a corn mill known as Forge Mill.

But it was not just the main river channel that was being utilised to generate power for industrial workings. Four mills are recorded on Back Brook near Kington and a mill is marked on the 1754 map at Moor Court on Curl Brook. All of the mills are now disused and are of varying states of disrepair. However some of the land and mill owners are looking into restoring these buildings. The mill at Staunton-on -Arrow is a particularly fine example and much of the workings remain in place which is in contrast to the regrettable removal of machinery when these buildings are converted to residential use.

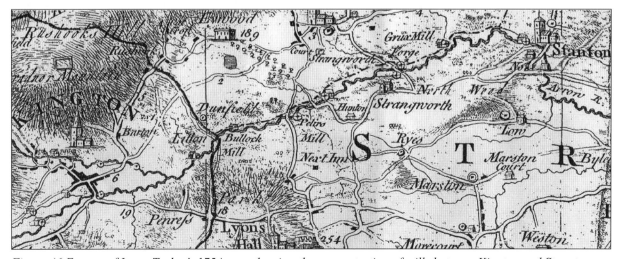

Figure 46 Extract of Isaac Taylor's 1754 map showing the concentration of mills between Kington and Staunton

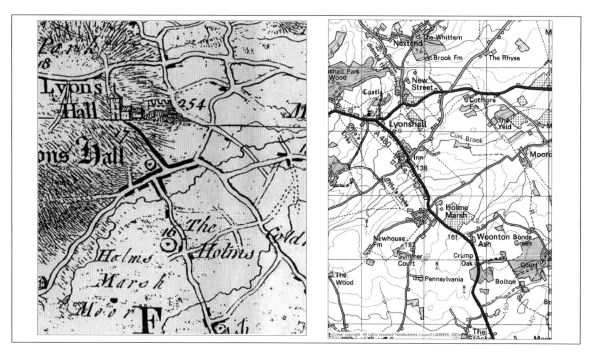

Figure 47 Changes in the routeways around Lyonshall village between 1754 and today. Also note the inaccurate location of Lyonshall church and castle on the earlier map.

However it is known from the field survey and farm surveys carried out as part of the present AVALCC project that water management features can be observed along the entirety of the Arrow Valley. The location of which could be cross- referenced to the first edition Ordnance Survey maps. This is discussed further in the next chapter on how the landscape has been farmed.

Routeways

One aspect of change in the historic environment that we were was keen to capture in the project was how communications, in particular the road network, had altered and how this reflects the movement of people around the landscape. The level of 'accessibility' to the routeways varies considerably, from being retained as a road to downgrading to a public footpath through fields or to total abandonment. It is possible, however, that many routes were never more than a dirt track across fields in the first place.

As with other elements of the historic environment such as trees and woodland, the accuracy and detail upon the earliest maps vary considerably. For example, no roads are recorded in and around Huntington or Kington Rural on Taylor's 1754 map. On the 1789 map by Carey many of the roads shown

on Taylor's map do not appear. Carey's map seems to have an unfinished quality about it as far as mapping roads are concerned. Junctions of roads are marked on the map but the line of the road is started and is just left going to nowhere. Another problem was that without accurate surveying techniques used by the mapmakers a road that is marked on all the maps can vary considerably in direction and it becomes difficult to assess which road is actually being represented. As this added more time to the analysis of the road system, certain areas were selected for analysis to highlight the potential of study. Each historical map was studied in broad areas to the west and east of Kington from Huntington to Staunton-on-Arrow.

In the area to the west of Kington many of the roads that must have existed are not marked and this suggeststhat the cartographers perceived this part of Herefordshire as being remote. One road that is mapped heads south from Huntington to the south-west of Knowl farm on the modern Brilley to Kington road. This still survives although as a bridleway in part across Burnt Bridge and Burnt Hengoed.

A road from Hergest Bridge to Mere Farm and Moseley Farm survives although the route has changed course in places. The line of the old road as seen on the 1754 map has survived in places as a public footpath. In fact many of the roads around Kingswood survive as public footpaths particularly around Pembers Oak. One road that did exist was the route from the south of Kington that ran along the northern fringe of Kingswood through what is now Newburn Farm and linked to the road over Hergest Bridge near Bredward. The majority of this routeway survives as a public right of way but it is marked on the earliest maps up to the 1830s as a major route towards Wales, by-passing the centre of Kington. It is at this point in time that New Barns, (now Newburn) appears as a named location on the map. The road on the northern side of the river Arrow appears to have developed at this time.

Very few roads are marked in Kingswood and it is not until the 19th century that the road from Kington to Ashfield/Ashmoor is marked and it is not until after the clearance of Kingswood after the 1850s that the road system, which we know today, is established. The Woodbrook to Kington road (A4111) only appears in 1832. Until then the route was from Penrhos along Jack's Ditch Lane. This route is not fully marked on the earliest maps and remains unclear until 1832 when roads and tracks are clearly marked in the Kingswood area. In 1832 the route along Jack's Ditch Lane to Woodbrook only goes as far as what is now called The Bungalow, near Oxpasture Wood. A road linking Woodbrook with Lyonshall through Lynhales and Rodds Wood also goes out of use by the 1830s. There are now no rights of way following these old routes on the modern maps.

To the east of Kington the road system has changed considerably. The Kington to Titley road has changed course just south of Eywood park. The earliest map of 1754, shows the road heading across what is now known as The Green, just south of Titley Pool. It crosses the avenue of trees at Eywood. By 1801 this has changed and the road follows the current layout. On the 1832 map the road is shown as going around the avenue of trees. This would seem to indicate that the emparkment of Eywood resulted in the changes in the road network due to private ownership. The route does however survive as a public footpath.

Taylor's and Bowen's maps (1754 and 1762) show a road from Barton to Rushock. This does not appear to have gone out of use until the 1880s. Although

the road on the Tithe map of 1845 for Kington shows the road from Rushock to Barton stopping at Barton and not continuing down to the modern B4355 as it had done on previous maps, it would suggest that it may have been going out of use. However on the 1852 map it appears to be the major route from Kington to Titley. The road is marked on the earliest maps as continuing past Rushock towards Eywood although it is hard to say where it ends up. On the 1754 map it ends up just south of Oat Croft which may be the modern Oakcroft Farm. On the 1832 Ordnance Survey map and the 1845 Kington and Titley Tithe maps it continues as shown to Golden Bank, but it does not continue on to Eywood as shown on the earlier maps. The 1852 map shows that this road is still in existence. By the 1880 Ordnance Survey map this network had largely gone out of existence. The road from Golden Bank does not continue on to Eywood. The Rushock to Barton route has by this time become a footpath.

There is also a road from Rushock down to Litton on the 1754 map. It is not fully marked on the 1762 map but is hinted at as a faint dashed line. The road is only marked on from Rushock to the B3455 on the 1801 map. In 1832 the road is marked from the B3455 down to what is now known as Mill farm. However the stretch of track from the B3455 to Rushock has gone. This part is shown on the 1885 Ordnance Survey map as a footpath. The lane down to Mill Farm shown on the 1885 Ordnance Survey map as Piers Grove Farm, is represented as a track. The modern route to Mill Farm follows part of the old track and what was a footpath on the 1885 Ordnance Survey map heading to what is now Lower Downfield. This old road is now the route of the Mortimer Trail, a public walking trial through northwest Herefordshire.

However it is not only roads that have changed. The 1832 and 1835 maps show the Kington Tram Road. It is shown heading from Burlingjobb, to the west of Kington, through Kington and down through Lyonshall Park. It curves south here and heads down through Castle Weir and Lyonshall. It continues past Almeley to Hay on Wye. This route is shown on the 1852 map, but by the 1880s it had gone out of use. The railways had superseded the tramway and only a small section of tramway is marked on the map in Lyonshall Park. The tramway is still recorded as a place-name however. A pond was created sometime between 1905 and 1930 and was called Tramway Pool. It is still there today and the line of the old tramway is followed in part by a modern road leading from Bullocks Mill through Lyonshall Park Wood to the A44.

Around Lyonshall the dense network of routes between Lyonshall village and Moor Court to the east has changed. The main change is a road that linked Bryncurl to Broxwood, three miles away (Figure 47). This traversed the landscape crossing Curl Brook to Cold Heart and continued in a south-easterly direction to Sour Brook and onto the crossroads which is located to the south of Broxwood Park. The stretch between Bryncurl and Cold Heart survives as a public footpath while the section between Cold Heart and Sourbrook Farm has disappeared but is marked as a field boundary. Between Sourbrook and Broxwood it remains as a roadway.

In comparison to the Lyonshall area, Staunton-on-Arrow has experienced a limited gain in the network of routeways through history. The road between Staunton and Burcher near Titley via Horseway Head is not on the earliest maps and does not appear until 1832. At Stansbatch there was a crossroads with the southern road running from Stansbatch to Lower Mowley. This survives as a public footpath today but appears by the beginning of the 20th century to have declined in status and the main east-west route through Stansbatch from Stockley Cross dominated the routeway.

This brief study of the communication system shows how much information can be retrieved from historical maps and points to some potential directions for future work. It would be interesting for instance to gauge the whole extent of change by measuring the distances of loss or gain on a parish basis. The date and possible reasons for such change could possibly be cross- referenced to historical documents that may explain changes in land ownership for example, or changes in land management.

Historical sites

As already mentioned within this report the historical sites that are most recognisable in the Arrow Valley include Iron Age hillforts, Rowe Ditch, Offa's Dyke and the medieval castles. The earliest cartographers acknowledged the existence of these ancient sites to a varying degree. The Iron Age hillforts at Wapley Hill and Ivington Camp are marked on Taylor's 1754 map with the subsequent extent of the Wapley Hill fortifications marked on later maps apart from Cary's 1801 map. It is not until the 1832 Ordnance Survey map that the cartographers change from symbolic representations of the hillfort to actually mapping the physical extent of the elaborate earthworks present on both sites. Other features included a Tumulus recorded to the south of Strangwood (now called Strangworth) in 1832 and a tump at The Whittern, Lyonshall in 1835.

The line and extent of Rowe Ditch is recorded on the earliest map of 1754 demonstrating its dominance in the low-lying landscape of the river valley. What is of interest is the difference in the length between what is recorded on this map and what is extant as an earthwork today. It is recorded as running from the south of Woodhouse to the west of Milton House and continues in a continuous line past what was to become Pitfield Farm and onto Bearwood Common to the southeast of Pembridge. However it is not until the 1832 map that it is recorded again where its length is considerably shorter, only running from the south of the Milton Cross - Stansbatch road to the former Bagley Lane. On the 1835 Bryant map it is marked extending beyond Bagley Lane and continuing over the southern side of the river to Pitfield Farm and this represents the current interpretation of its known entire length.

Unlike Rowe Ditch, the existence of Offa's Dyke within the county is not marked on a map until the 1832 Ordnance Survey map. The extent of the surviving earthworks that are mapped at that time appear to be generally the same as what is still visible in the landscape today. The only difference is that the 1832 map might suggest it surviving to the south of Berry's Wood, Titley. This appears to be confirmed by Bryant's map and it is suggested that the earthworks runs continuously from the south of Eywood Park, Titley to Holme Marsh, Lyonshall.

The Medieval castles are recorded upon the maps of the Arrow Valley. Huntington, Kington and Lyonshall are all recorded on the earliest maps. An issue of accuracy in the mapping is raised where it was realised that the castle and church at Lyonshall are recorded on the southern side of the Kington-

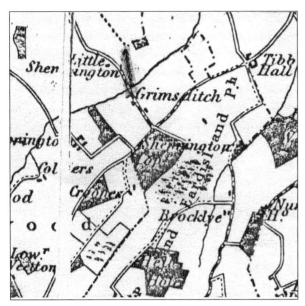

Figure 48 Extract of Bryant's 1835 map of Herefordshire showing the historical feature of Grimsditch, near Little Sherrington in the southern part of Pembridge parish

Pembridge road (Figure 47). This mistake continues up to Bryant's map and it is not until the Ordnance Survey of 1832 that it is located in its correct position to the north of the Kington - Pembridge road. The smaller castles within the Arrow valley are not recorded until a later date. The 'Turret' located between Huntington and Huntington Lodge and Castle Twts was not recorded until 1832 while the motte and bailey castles or tumps at Hengoed and also in the parish of Huntington are not recorded until 1880s Ordnance Survey mapping.

Other features

One interesting aspect of studying earlier maps is the recording of historical sites that can no longer be seen within the landscape and without these historical maps would be lost to the knowledge of an area. The earliest map by Taylor records 'camps' at two locations. One is located at Bradnor Mountain, Kington and another to the west of Burton Court, Eardisland. At both sites it is difficult to define any sort of earthwork that can be observed today. This is perhaps not surprising, certainly at Bradnor Hill which is now the site of a golf course. There was no doubt that a substantial amount of earth was moved in order to create the course itself which possibly destroyed the site before it could be recorded in accordance with modern archaeological standards. Similarly at Burton Court, members of the Eardisland Oral History Group have

noted the bulldozing and landscaping of the area of the presumed camp at a place called Admarsh Coppice during the 1970s.

Finally an interesting feature upon Bryant's 1835 map is a small stretch of earthwork known as Grimsditch (Figure 48). This feature is recorded as a placename on the earlier maps to the south of Luntley Court but appears to move westwards towards Sherrington Manor by 1832 and is marked on the map as a building. Located on the parish boundary between Pembridge and Dilwyn it is marked by Bryant as an earthwork similar to Rowe Ditch. It has been postulated whether this linear earthwork might have been a continuation of Rowe Ditch and therefore represents the fragmented remnants of its most southern- most extent (Hill and Worthington, 2003). An excavation at its presumed location at what is now called Little Sherrington, near Tibbet's Brook, revealed no obvious evidence for the existence of this feature (*ibid*).

Perhaps it should also be pointed out that none of these sites are recorded by the Ordnance Survey, whose staff produced such detailed mapping of the country and recorded the landscape in such detail. It could be argued that perhaps these features did not actually exist in the first place and their appearance upon the maps was based upon local legends or folklore. Equally perhaps these sites did exist and due to erosion these features were removed from the visible landscape.

7.4 Landscape history from the pattern of enclosure

The most recent approach to studying landscape change involves a process of characterising the modern day landscape in historical terms. This involves studying the mapped boundaries and field systems and deducing their historical origins and the rate of change that has occurred within an area of landscape.

This source of information recently developed is the Historic Landscape Characterisation project (Ray and White, 2004). During 1999- 2000 English Heritage funded Herefordshire Archaeology to undertake a study of mapping the current landscape in terms of the historical origin and development.

Broad phases can be observed from the very earliest enclosures through to the more recent 'survey-planned' landscapes of the 17th Century onwards. Those areas that appear to retain an early form of landscape organisation or where the field pattern has captured the former landscape organisation of the medieval period and earlier has been termed *retentive* (*see the glossary for the definition of terms used*). Those areas that are dominated by a geometric shaped field pattern and straight boundaries have been defined as *survey- planned* and probably date from the post- medieval and reflect interest in land improvement, estate management and the development of cartography and survey during this period. These two broad phases can be seen as representing opposite ends of the enclosed landscape, while in between there are what have been characterised as *adaptive* landscapes, where enclosures and field patterns contain elements of organisation that can be considered both retentive and survey- planned. Figure 49 shows the map of the Arrow Valley in terms of its historic landscape character.

As the River Arrow enters Herefordshire the landscape to the west of Kington is dominated by a distinctive field pattern, that demanded an historical interpretation. Along the southern facing slopes of Hergest Ridge the boundaries consist of sinuous linear features that demarcate broadly rectangular fields. These boundaries have been established on a north west to south east orientation (Figure 50). The form and regularity of this field pattern over such a wide area of landscape suggests a large- scale organisation that, if compared with similar patterns in other areas of Britain, may likewise date from the prehistoric period (Fleming, 1988; Williamson, 1987). These major axial land-divisions may have been in place by the end of the Bronze Age (c. 1000-800 BC). However, the areas between such boundaries were divided – in places – into fields on a piecemeal basis, probably during the Iron Age. Exactly the same orientation of field boundaries is seen again around Lyonshall village and this appears to set the orientation for later historical features such as Offa's Dyke and the village of Lyonshall itself. This area stretches along the Curl Brook from Weston to the south of Kingswood.

Between these two areas of possible early field systems are areas that have experienced re-organisation. Around Kington, the co-axial system

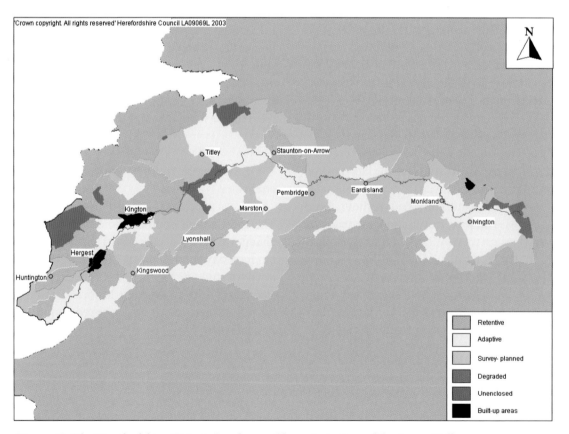

Figure 49 The Herefordshire Historic Landscape Characterisation of the Arrow Valley

Figure 50 Aerial photograph of the co-axial field boundaries in the Arrow Valley to the southeast of Kington.
©WNFC/MASH 00-C-0734

is interrupted with survey- planning of boundaries and the insertion of straight field boundaries. These form larger geometric shaped fields that in comparison to the earlier system disregard the topography of the landscape. Also there is the distinct area of the enclosure of Kingswood. The area defined by this enclosure of smallholdings and rectangular fields mirrors exactly the boundary of the woodland at Kingswood during the mid-19th century very accurately.

Further downstream there are possible indications of the co-axial pattern continuing but the pattern has been again disrupted by medieval common arable fields and the 'straightening' of boundaries during the post- medieval period. The excavations carried out as part of this AVALCC project at The Leen would suggest that the field pattern around area of fields around Rowe Ditch was established during the Romano- British period. Although the field pattern appears to be derived from an axial pattern the orientation is different to the areas upstream near Kington. This may indicate different phases of organisation in the landscape, from prehistoric to Roman. Although it is too early to be certain of this, it does indicate an area for future research.

Indicators of medieval common arable fields can be identified along the valley. Within the field boundaries of today, 'dog-leg' kinks in field boundaries and narrower strips defined by hedges indicate clearly the piecemeal creation of a bounded landscape from formerly open fields.

From the east of Eardisland to its confluence with the Lugg the historic character of the Arrow Valley landscape is dominated by the gradual adaptation of the enclosure of former common arable fields on the higher ground that surrounds the valley floor and the enclosure of former meadow on the valley floor itself.

A recent study of the Parliamentary enclosures in Herefordshire has revealed that the Arrow Valley was subject to very limited enclosure from this process (Farquhar-Oliver, 2003). In fact the whole county was subject to very small impact of the Act of Parliamentary enclosure (Grey, 1915). This process of enclosure mainly dates from the late 18th century and continued into the late 19th century. The areas of landscape that were often enclosed were former 'open' common arable fields or areas described as 'waste' which consisted of rough upland grazing or lowland commons. Five distinct areas of Parliamentary enclosure have been defined by Farquhar-Oliver within the Arrow Valley.

These areas correspond exactly with the areas defined by the Historic Landscape Characterisation as areas of survey-planned enclosure. The clearest comparisons are at Huntington and Kingswood where the Historic Landscape Characterisation areas defined are the same in extent as the Parliamentary enclosure while the enclosure awards downstream are located within broad areas of landscape change in particular at Bearswood Common to the southwest of Pembridge.

The study of the modern farmed landscape which has been carried out as part of the Historic Landscape Characterisation shows that much of the landscape was laid out at a potentially early time possibly as early as the Late Iron Age. It is not suggested that the actual hedgerows date to that period but that the organisation of the landscape has been inherited, adapted but respected from generation to generation. This has lead to the patchwork of intricate field patterns that contribute so much to the historic character of the Arrow Valley.

Chapter summary: some key points

- Land-use in the Arrow Valley can be 'profiled' from the period of the earliest maps in the late sixteenth and seventeenth centuries. This reveals that the upper part of the Arrow Valley within Herefordshire had more arable up to the nineteenth century than it has had since then.

- Early maps can be used to make observations about former settlement patterns, the extent and nature of woodland and tree cover, the form and distribution of ornamental parkland, the existence of mills and water management features, the pattern of communications, and the character of a range of other features.

- Deductions for the Arrow Valley about the extent of former woodland (before extensive conifer plantations) and about routeways, is particularly enlightening. Network change and the 'growth of privacy' are particularly noticeable when looking at tracks, lanes and roads in the landscape of two hundred years ago, compared with today.

- Study of the pattern of enclosure itself reveals a heritage of 'survey – planning' of the landscape in the period 1700 to 1850. While this included areas of former woodland or waste, much of it comprised the reorganisation of the landscape into straight-sided fields as part of a general trend in agricultural improvement.

- While the 'latest' enclosures are recent in date, there are indications right down the Arrow Valley for an establishment of field systems on a northwest to southeast orientation as far back as perhaps 1000 BC.

Chapter 8

How the landscape has been farmed

8.1 Introduction

An important element of the AVALCCP was the survey of farms and landholdings. The purpose of this was twofold. Firstly, the aim was to conduct a walk- over survey of the holding accompanied by the farmer or landowner to recognise any features that might relate to the historic environment. Secondly it provided an opportunity to listen to a personal account of how the landscape has changed in terms of its general management, the reasons for that change and for the owner to describe any historical features or artefacts they have noticed or come across upon their landholding. It was considered important to get a perspective on the changes on land management from those who are responsible for such changes and to record the oral history of how the landscape has changed certainly during the latter part of the twentieth century.

The farm visits comprised of a rapid walkover survey followed by the systematic observation of historical features. This was undertaken where possible with a hand held Global Positioning System (GPS). Particular attention was paid to evidence for historic water management within each landholding. Where it was feasible, the farmer or landowner accompanied the surveyor, and this provided an opportunity to gain information en-route concerning the history of land use. The success of this survey was only possible through the kind co- operation of the landowners/ farmers to permit access onto the land and to devoting half a day or even more in some cases to accompanying one of the surveyors. We are therefore grateful to all those farmers and owners who committed their time to the project. A report on each of the individual farms has been prepared and will be given to each of the farmers or landowners (Renfrew, 2003a- g; White, 2003d- i; White and Renfrew, 2003b). This chapter describes the historical features that were recorded as part of the farm surveys.

8.2 A profile of the whole farm surveys

In total 14 farms were surveyed during the tight timescale of the project. These varied in size from the smallest of just over 7 acres at Little Broome, Eardisland to 750 acres at Broadward Hall, Leominster. The average acreage of the surveyed farms was 265 acres with the surveyed farms being located along the valley in the different reaches of the River Arrow. In total over 3700 acres were surveyed as part of the project. The intention was to structure the sample of farm holdings based upon their location in the river valley, whether upland or lowland and by the type of farming regime whether the farm is within a Countryside Stewardship Scheme, or has obtained Organic status or subject to no management agreements.

Based upon a walkover survey the historical features that could be seen were mainly earthworks. The majority of these features relate to former landscape organisation, landuse or settlement. However there were also indications of other features that may relate to the prehistoric period. It should be pointed out that almost all of the observed features are not on public rights of way and the recording of such features does not provide a right to access the land on which these sites are recorded. Permission should always be obtained from the landowner.

At The Leen, Pembridge two mounds were observed in the neighbouring fields to Milton Cross where a group of prehistoric burial mounds is known. These mounds at The Leen may in fact be the previously unrecorded remains of prehistoric barrows and form part of the original cemetery. These barrows are difficult to see as they stand less than 0.5 metres in height and have spread to approximately 18 metres in diameter. Apart from this example the majority of observations related to the earthwork remains of the earlier organisation of the landscape and this could be seen on many of the farms visited.

Curving earthworks of the headlands between medieval fields can still be seen in the pasture fields around Rowe Ditch. At the Lowe Farm former field boundaries survive as very shallow banks and ditches and in places appear to be cut by water management channels implying that these field boundaries predate the water system (Figure 51). The best preserved earthworks of medieval field systems were found around Titley at Lower Mowley

Figure 51 Aerial photograph looking east along the Arrow Valley with The Lowe Farm in the foreground.
© HAAS 03-CN-0610

and Newburn Farm, Kington. Ridge and furrow from medieval ploughing survives within the pasture fields while on the higher slopes of the river valley, lynchets could be observed. On other farms the hedged boundaries are planted along the line of the medieval ploughing furlongs as at Court House Farm and to the north of the farmhouse at Luntley.

Very straight ridges could be seen surviving at Folly Farm, The Lowe, The Leen Court House Farm (Eardisland) and Woodbrook Farm. This may relate to the establishment of orchards rather than to medieval ploughing due to the straightness of the earthworks and the proximity of these features to the farmhouse. At Woodbrook Farm, Kingswood Susan Bowen showed the author where the boundary between Kingswood and Moseley Common used to be. This division between the two different areas still survives as a low bank located beneath a hedgerow on the farm and is now incorporated into the wider landscape enclosure pattern.

An old holloway between the fields can still be seen crossing the fields at Newburn Farm and would have provided access to Kingswood, situated above the farm. The location of this holloway was compared to the maps that had been studied, and this revealed that the routeway had not been marked onto early maps. This may suggest by the time of the mid 18th Century the track had gone out of use. Former routeways could also be seen at Luntley Court where the routeway is preserved as a field boundary, and at The Leen a small section of the Bagley Lane survives to the west of Rowe Ditch.

The remnants of buildings and former settlements were seen in the corners of fields on many of the farms. At Luntley the plock or garden around what would have been a dwelling survives between Tippet's Brook and the roadway. Flat rectangular areas were observed also at Grove Farm, Broom, The Lowe, The Leen and Court of Noke. All have been interpreted as building platforms. This illustrates the extent of settlement and population change in the rural landscape. Caution should always be taken when interpreting earthworks and

Figure 52 Enlargement of aerial photograph showing the network of ditches recorded as part of a whole farm survey at Luntley. ©HAAS 03-CN-1714

this was illustrated by Hugh Lowe of Court House Farm in Eardisland. An area of irregular earthworks upon his farm actually relates to the dumping of silt from the moat around the castle mound in Eardisland during the 19th century and again in 1974.

Within Titley Park the remains of a previously unrecorded pillow mound has been detected in the corner of the parkland. Also indicators of woodland management were recognised around the ornamental ponds where a charcoal burning platform had been cut by the channel created for the pond. This indicates the likelihood that woodland industry was occurring in this area prior to the formal establishment of the parkland.

An aspect of the farm profile was to assess from the landowners perspective how the farm has changed to respond to external demand and pressures since they have been farming there. In all but one of the farms visited as part of the project the emphasis of farm management has changed from pasture to an arable production and in some cases the amount of land-use that has changed is over a third in less than ten years. Also there has been a decline in the labour force with less people being

employed with leasing of land and the use of contractors a factor on virtually every farm holding. All of this relates to the economic conditions and the scale of the work involved in running the farms. This does have implications for the survival of these earthworks for the future. In fact the change to ploughing has already resulted in the removal of some historical features such as settlement and building platforms and old routeways the location of which have been shared with us by the landowners and farmers involved in the project. This project has provided an opportunity to record some of the historical features upon some of the farms but also to hear about the knowledge that exists about the landscape from those who work the land.

8.3 The work of drainage and water management

The use of water for milling and industry has already been highlighted as part of the map regression work but the utilisation of water did not stop there. There remains evidence of water meadows, that could be deliberately flooded, and the associated sluices and weirs. When do water meadows date from? The development of water meadows appears to date from the late 16th and 17th centuries. Water meadows are noted as early as 1582/3 in the parish of Eyton to the north of Leominster in the Lugg Valley (Edwards, 1991) and there is no reason why they could not have existed at the same time in the Arrow Valley. The meadows could be flooded during the winter months to protect the grass from harsh frosts and provide nutrients from the silts to support a good harvest the following year.

The oral historical information gained on how the river and drainage system had been used in the past was extremely interesting. For instance, there are stories about how cattle used to be watered and how channels could be dammed in order to dip sheep. Stories also exist about the straightening of stream channels and the location of a fishery upstream of Eardisland. Throughout the valley there are indications of water management not just on the main river channel of the Arrow but even on the smallest of tributaries.

For instance, in Huntington parish, a large leat can still be seen running off a tributary of the Gladestry Brook in the field behind the village hall that used to feed the fishpond next to the castle. Also a leat can be seen traversing the contours of the hillslope

to the southwest of Penllan. This is associated with the remains of a stone lined weir or sluice across a small brook which feeds into the Arrow.

Along the Curl Brook near Pembridge the remains of water channels across the fields can be seen to the east of Marston Court. Between Moseley Common and Lowe Farm the course of the brook has been straightened. This was, according to Clive Williams of The Lowe, to prevent the continual changing of the stream channel which had changed and caused disagreement between the different landowners, during the earlier part of the twenieth century, that one was gaining land while the other side was losing land. A similar stretch of channel straightening can also be observed at Luntley Court Farm. Also around Luntley Court Farm are well-preserved ditches on the northern side of Tippet's Brook. The owner, David Owens, remembers the flooding of these meadows through these drainage ditches. A square platform area created by some of the ditches (that here are nearly one metre deep in places) may define the location of a moated homestead. This is located opposite the existing farmhouse and Court buildings in a corner of the field. One side of this platform is sited parallel with the Luntley to Bearwood road (Figure 52).

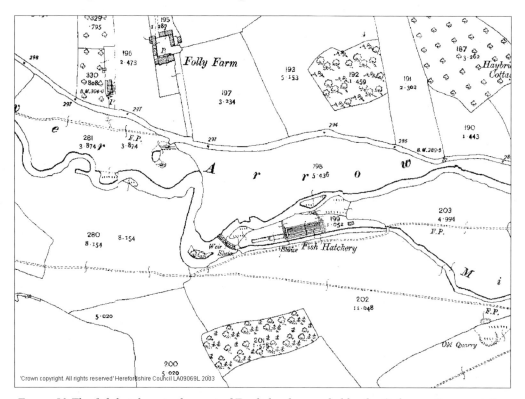

Figure 53 The fish hatchery to the west of Eardisland, recorded by the Ordnance Survey at the turn of the 20th Century

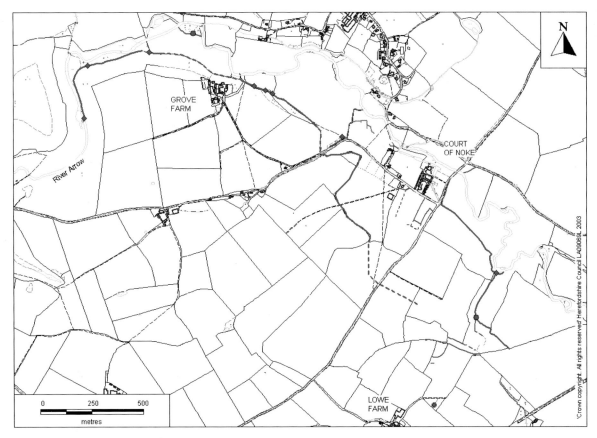

Figure 54 The extensive earthwork leats of a water management system that starts at Grove Farm and continues onto other landholdings.

Upstream of Eardisland at Folly Farm, in the field called Weir Patch there used to be a small fishery (Figure 53). This was a short- lived feature dating to the beginning of the 20ᵗʰ century but unfortunately, the earthworks were bulldozed approximately 25 years ago. All that remains is the weir on the river channel (which also acts as the weir to the Eardisland mills) and the feeder leat to the mill and former fishery. The sluices that controlled the supply of water to the fishery have been removed. Likewise by Court House Farm in Eardisland the mill race survives, sluice gates with eel traps are recorded at Glanarrow and Arrow Mill.

At Newburn Farm near Kington, river meadows were flooded during winter months on the southern side of the river. The main central drain appears to survive as a wide shallow ditch. The mill races that supplied water to the Kington mills are recorded on the Tithe maps and on the Ordnance Survey maps. They can still be observed and survive in good condition. A feature that had not been previously recorded here or mapped was an outflow or overflow system that survives in parts. Drainage for water meadows can be observed at Broom and Little Broome surviving along the edges of fields. These fields were supplied from the water system of Staunton-on-Arrow at Milton Cross and from the system at Twyford.

In two different reaches of the Arrow the existence of more elaborate water management systems were recorded as part of the project. The first is located in the north- western corner of Pembridge parish between The Grove and the Court of Noke and the second at Broadward Hall, downstream from Ivingtonbury in Leominster parish. Although the existence of these historical water features was already established, this project provided the opportunity for their visible extent and condition to be mapped for the first time (Figure 54 and 57). What is also of interest are the differences between the water management regimes. At The Grove the contour and hillslope along the river valley was used to facilitate the transport of water. Meanwhile in the flatter landscape of Broadward the builders

Figure 55 Remains of a stone sluice gate survives near the River Arrow as part of the leat system that starts at The Grove.

relied upon a process of blocking and diverting river flow using carefully located leats.

The leat at The Grove starts downstream of The Forge. What is remarkable is that it feeds water to a number of different farms along the river valley from The Grove, Court of Noke and The Lowe before returning to the main river channel by The Leen (Figure 54). The main channel can still be traced in the landscape for over one and half miles and survives in places up to one metre in depth. On the land belonging to The Grove different types of sluice gates could still be seen along the course of the leat. In two places the sluice to flood the meadow fields was no more than a gap in the leat which could be opened or blocked with a large plank of wood. More substantial sluices made from stone were visible that appear to form an overflow system that allowed water to be returned back to the main river through dug channels (Figure 55). Fields were still being flooded by this method up to the late 1930's.

The leat from The Grove then crosses underneath Noke Lane and enters the land belonging to Court of Noke. From the farm and field survey, it is unclear what then happens to the course of the leat. It appears to branch in two, with the main channel working its way towards The Lowe while the other channel continues towards the Court of Noke and possibly returning to the river by Noke Bridge. This channel continues along the contour of the slope and through a series of boltholes that could be used to flood the meadows through a series of channels. The secondary channel appears subsequently to have been widened and used as an access track up

the field before turning along Noke Lane, and possibly connecting back to the river at some point near to Noke Bridge. The fields on the opposite side of the road to the Court of Noke buildings contain well preserved ditches that form part of the larger flooding system (Figure 56). At The Lowe, an extensive network of leats survive along the field boundaries up to a depth of 0.7 metres and return water across the southern part of The Leen farmholding back to the River Arrow.

At Broadward Hall the water management system is impressive and forms part of the wider network of leats that criss-cross this part of the landscape. These are best preserved on the southern side of the river and survive as ditches up to 1 metre in depth and 3 metres wide. The networks of leats are extensive in scale here and could be mapped over four separate fields (Figure 57). However no form of sluice gate or weirs could be seen that would indicate how the supply of water to the various channels could have been regulated.

Figure 56 Aerial photograph of the elaborate earthwork banks situated next to the River Arrow between The Grove and Court of Noke.

©HAAS 03-CN-1328

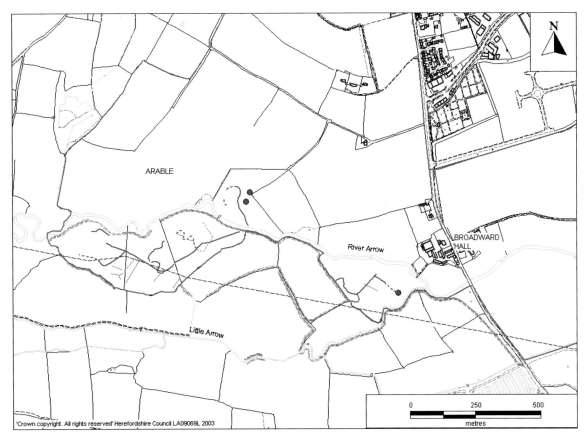

ARABLE

River Arrow

BROADWARD HALL

Little Arrow

| 0 | 250 | 500 |

metres

Figure 57 The mapped remains of the water meadow system that survives at Broadward Hall, to the south of Leomunster near to the confluence of the River Arrow with the River Lugg

It was noted at Broom, Eardisland that the construction of the railway line had disrupted the former drainage channels on the northern side of the river valley and this altered the drainage pattern within the immediate area. This ultimately limited the access of water to the farm holding. One of the greatest impacts upon the continuation and use of water meadows during the 20th century was the two World Wars.

The impact of the loss of so many lives during the First World War saw the number of men employed at Ivingtonbury for instance greatly reduced and resulted in the decline in the use of the water meadows then. Working and maintaining water meadows is labour intensive and reflects a time when the countryside was more densely populated and employment was derived almost exclusively from agriculture. However the system at Ivingtonbury can still be observed in the pasture fields. Careful management by the current owner is safeguarding these remains for future generations. During the Second World War, many areas of former pasture were ploughed up for the war effort to provide food and sustain the population. Speaking to farmers on how farming has changed it was noted that it was during the war that the first tractors were brought onto the farm, replacing horse drawn ploughs.

More recently the pressures on pasture fields near to the river channel that contain the remains of water meadows have come from the intensification of agriculture, and in particular arable farming, since the 1970s. This has sadly often seen the levelling of the earthworks associated with past water management. On the farms along the valley that were surveyed the leats were located in the centre of the fields or cut diagonally across the field. This made ploughing problematical and many of the leats had been filled in. In some places drainage was still necessary and the channel was diverted to the edge of the field. Examples of this were noted at Titley Court and The Leen. Tony Norman of The Leen Farm explained another reason why the leats were backfilled during this time. From the 1970s, many parts of the river valley were attached to mains water. This meant that cattle could be provided drinking water straight from the tap rather than drinking out of the leats or field drains. This prevented the infection of the cattle with liver fluke and the consequent reduction in the value of the stock. Supplying water troughs and filling in the old leats provided the most logical option of preventing the disease from persisting.

Chapter Summary: Some key points

- A series of 14 whole farm surveys revealed a variety of features surviving as earthworks and varying in date from the Bronze Age to the twentieth century. Other earthwork remains included clear traces of medieval and other early ploughlands.

- The most detailed information gained, and a deliberate focus for study, concerned the earthworks and evidence for water management systems.

- Important remains of early over watering systems were traced in a number of locations. At five farms significant water systems were mapped but a particularly important series were noted in interconnecting farms on the borders of Pembridge and Staunton-on-Arrow parishes, while a particularly well-preserved series survive between Ivingtonbury and Broadward near Leominster.

- The countryside was more densely settled than today with the majority of people working in agriculture. Changes in society and the rural economy have seen the abandonment of the earlier water networks and flood meadow systems.

Chapter 9

Registering change in the landscape

9.1 Introduction

The two preceding chapters have indicated how landscape change can be studied by looking at historic maps and by listening to the oral history of residents within the Arrow Valley. But is it possible to create indicators of cumulative landscape change that gauge the effect of different activities on the historic environment? Up to now the work on landscape change has been retrospective - assessing what has happened in the past. There is also a need however to try and understand what the possible consequences of change in the future might be.

Unlike map regression study, nonetheless, there is no established methodology for examining such processes. There are no established 'indicators' whereby the ongoing processes of landscape change can be monitored. This is a question that is central to the definition of this study as concerning itself with landscape change and conservation. The series of indices outlined in this chapter, as the way of trying to characterise landscape change involved, are therefore exploratory, and unapologetically so. They represent a local 'first step' in addressing these important issues.

On the one hand, in this project they have been based on landscape characterisation of a fairly impressionistic nature. And yet, on the other hand, the observations reported have been supported by a systematic study of the landscape on a field by field basis, that has involved noting key landscape characteristics (eg hedgerow, field trees) and an estimation of the 'erosive' regime resulting from current and recent land use.

9.2 Landscape character and change

Before we can register change in the landscape, we need to specify its character. Recently there have been two studies into the character of the Herefordshire landscape. These are the Landscape Character Assessment undertaken by the former County Council of Hereford and Worcester and completed by Herefordshire Council; and the English Heritage supported Historic Landscape Characterisation that was completed by Herefordshire Archaeology.

The Herefordshire Landscape Character Assessment specifies the character of the landscape primarily in visual terms, that reflect the geology, topography and ecology of a landscape area. By visiting various areas of the landscape the parameters listed above, and more, were categorised into dominant, apparent or insignificant depending upon the surveyors' interpretation of the surrounding landscape. Sources of change were also recorded, for instance changes in settlement pattern, possible changes in land- use such as mineral extraction or forestry.

The Historic Landscape Characterisation maps the landscape in terms of its historical origins and development and is based upon the interpretation of the enclosure pattern from recent maps (Ray and White, 2004). It is possible to register broad- brush areas of change in the landscape based upon the principles that the landscape is a constant that continually adapts and that change occurs at a different rate across the county. Consequently, it is possible to distinguish between the different historic landscape character areas and therefore register for instance modern changes within the landscape such as the creation of larger fields through the removal of hedgerows.

The field pattern of an area is just one of the elements of the landscape that contributes to its local distinctiveness (Figure 58). Much of this local distinctiveness is derived from historic features such as field boundaries or the buildings of a region. It is therefore important to try and register the local distinctiveness and to note existing changes to these elements and define possible changes that may occur in the future. One element that we were keen to investigate was not only the form of and changes to field boundaries but the nature of the vegetation that the enclosure boundary is constructed from.

Another element is the built heritage of an area. The building materials,especially those used for the walls and roof, as well as the useage of buildings, can contribute to the character of an area. Changes to any of the attributes of the building can alter the character not only of the building but also its relationship to the surrounding landscape. Beyond

Figure 58 The distictive landscape and enclosure pattern around Huntington looking towards Kington.
© HAAS 03-CN-0536

individual buildings another aspect of local distinctiveness is the density and size of buildings that make up the various farm complexes dotted along the valley. No previous work is known to exist in this area which has looked into how farm buildings have altered through time and the potential impact this may have had upon the character of the farm itself and the surrounding landscape.

Finally the role of agriculture and land use in the definition of the local character is important. Again, registering broad changes may reveal trends in the nature of change more generally within the Arrow Valley and the rate of change that has occured. Each of these elements of local distinctiveness is examined in more detail below.

9.3 Local distinctiveness: Boundaries

It is a truism that the landscape has radically altered during the last century. This change in the landscape is attributed in a large measure to the loss of hedgerows and field boundaries resulting from the intensification of arable farming. The analysis of

mapped changes in the field systems during this period should therefore enable us to gauge the extent of this change. The most obvious source for this information is the Ordnance Survey maps. The six miles to one inch maps of the 1880's provide an accurate coverage for the county which can be compared to the most recent epoch of mapping that is computerised within a Geographic Information System. The advantage of using computers is that it is possible to rapidly compare differences by overlaying each map of onto each other. As already established (see section 7.3) field boundaries can record within the enclosure pattern the historical organisation of the landscape. The wholesale removal of boundaries can lead to the degradation of this established pattern in the landscape.

Due to the pressure of time on this pilot project it was not possible to fully quantify the extent of change in boundaries from the 1880s to 2000 maps. It was nonetheless possible to document some general trends within the landscape project and the observations noted here are based upon each of the parishes.

It was noticed that the areas around Huntington and Kington Rural had not altered significantly and in fact the field pattern has virtually remained the same over at least the past 200 years. There was also limited boundary loss through Lyonshall with a small concentration of boundary loss detectable to the east of The Whittern. Here square shaped fields have been enlarged into rectangular fields by the systematic removal of interconnecting boundaries. There has been considerable significant boundary loss on the hill slopes above Titley between Green Lane Farm and Burcher. Enclosures here were doubled in size by the removal of boundaries. The area along the river at Titley has also seen the removal of boundaries in the area between the railway bridge and Bullock's Mill.

Some of the most substantial boundary loss can be observed within Pembridge parish. To the east of Broxwood Court the removal of field boundaries has resulted in eight separate fields becoming a single large field, which appears distinctively out of character with its surrounding landscape. A similar area can be observed to the south of Marston Court.

Between Staunton on Arrow and Rowe Ditch there has been significant boundary loss but this has not affected the overall character of the enclosure pattern. The relatively narrow rectangular fields that existed here have been expanded. However it is felt that if the process of boundary removal continued the historic character of the enclosure would be lost. Loss of boundaries or field pattern is matched in some places by the establishment of a new field pattern. For instance in the northernmost area of Pembridge parish around Milton, the field boundaries have been reorganised into large geometric fields that replaced the former sinuous boundaries that defined the enclosure. The enclosure of Bearwood Common in the west of Pembridge parish during the 19th Century produced a patchwork of small geometric orchards and paddocks located next to smallholdings. There has been a limited removal of boundaries within this pattern but the overall character of the area established then has remained intact.

Figure 59 Comparison of boundary change around Ivington Green, Leominster between the 1880s first edition Ordnance Survey and the modern map

The remains of the enclosure of former common arable fields that appeared to enclose individual strips have been removed to the east of Lower Hardwick. The narrow strips have been enlarged into sub- rectangular closes and fields. The removal of one or two boundaries that had subdivided the landscape into relatively small fields seems to be the general trend within the Arrow Valley. The result of the removal of these boundaries is the doubling in size of the field and the reduction in time spent in transferring agricultural machinery between fields. However it is not just old field systems that are subject to this. To the west of Ivington Court a distinct geometric grid pattern of field boundaries that sits on the interfluve between Stretford Brook and Honey Brook on the 1880s Ordnance Survey map has now been enlarged into singular rectangular fields, but the principal dividing boundaries between each field have been retained (Figure 59).

The documentation of boundary change demonstrates how dynamic changes in the rural landscape really are. A future study would hopefully measure distances and provide a quantifiable figure to the amount of change in the landscape since the time of accurate mapping of boundaries.

9.4 Trees and woodland

Oliver Rackham in his book *The History of the Countryside* asks the question 'How many farmland trees are there?'(Rackham, 1988). Rackham highlights here a very important point about obvious features in the landscape that have been and still are overlooked as an indicator of landscape change. The recording of trees in the landscape by archaeologists and historians has been neglected in the past but such trees are very much part of the cultural landscape since most have been deliberately planted or encouraged. The location of a tree within the landscape can inform us about how the processes by which the landscape may have changed. A tree situated in the centre of a field may signify the existence of an earlier enclosure boundary at such a location, for instance.

As noted in an earlier chapter, it is apparent when looking at maps of the Arrow Valley that there are in fact very few areas of woodland. However once one is actually standing in that mapped landscape, it is clear that the area possesses abundant tree cover.

These exist in the farmed landscape and in the past formed an important resource to the farmer. Evidence for this can be seen from the former pollarding of some of the hedgerow trees. In the past this provided timber for buildings and for other land uses such as poles for hopyards.

Within the limited scope and resources of this project it would have been impossible to count every tree or comment on its general management within the Arrow Valley. As part of the landscape survey rather than count the different trees an attempt was made therefore to characterise the nature of tree cover along the valley in terms of its overall visual appearance. Tree cover was divided into categories that included established hedgerows, the presence of trees within fields that may suggest former land divisions, and boundaries that contain a single species of hedging that may relate to a more systematic phase of landscape organisation.

Six separate categories were identified. Although it would have been impossible to count individual species of trees or note particular management, such as coppice or pollard, it was nonetheless possible to rapidly assess the general trend in tree cover. Hedges with multiple species and which were substantial in height or width were defined as 'established'. This implied that the enclosure boundary had been in existence for some time. Where only a single species hedge was present and appeared to have a straight form this was defined as 'quickset'. This suggested a recent reorganisation of the enclosed landscape. Other trees were noted such as veteran trees within hedgerows and trees possibly derived from park or woodland. If trees were situated in the middle of a field this might suggest the line of a former hedgerow.

Analysis of the data revealed that in the surveyed areas of the landscape nearly a quarter of the area consisted of enclosures where the tree cover was defined simply as 'established'. These areas were spread along the valley with no obvious pattern of distribution being recognised. When other tree cover patterns were noted within a land parcel the percentage of established hedges mixed with other tree cover rose to 72%. Over 52% of established hedges contained large veteran trees. This suggests that the enclosure boundaries within the Arrow Valley area of considerable longevity and have continued to be managed and adapted through time.

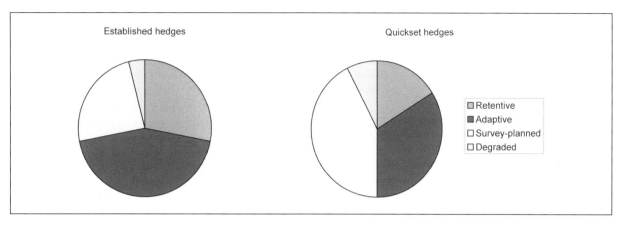

Figure 60 Comparison of type of hedge cover compared to the broad stratum of historic landscape character as defined by the Herefordshire Historic Landscape Characterisation

In contrast the number of land parcels solely defined by quickset hedges consisted of only 9% of the total number of land parcels surveyed within the area. This rises to 26% when noted as corresponding with other types of tree cover. 29% of quickset hedges have veteran trees associated with them and there is a distinct group with these characteristics within the landscape to the south and southwest of Lyonshall village that continues to Broxwood and to the south of Pembridge. This suggests a reorganisation of the landscape has taken place here, with the establishment of newer hedges possibly along the line of earlier hedges that needed to be laid. Fences with no tree cover characterise areas around Titley, Milton in northern Pembridge and to the south of Leominster. This reflects the land use of intensive grazing in pasture land and the need to stock- proof enclosures rapidly and relatively cheaply.

This work on the relationship of the types of tree cover to landscape development was supported by cross reference to the Historic Landscape Characterisation study results. Analysis of the type of tree cover and especially whether it was established or quickset, was compared to the broadest level of characterisation of landscape change as defined by the Herefordshire Historic Landscape Characterisation (Figure 60). This led to the observation that 28% of land parcels solely defined as possing established hedges were within the earliest ('retentive') stratum of the Historic Landscape Characterisation character area types. This rose to 44% for the 'adaptive' stratum before reducing to 24% for the historically more recent 'survey-planned' stratum. This suggests that although the 'adaptive' and 'survey- planned'

landscape character areas may be characterised by distinct geometric field patterns, there is an underlying 'history' of landscape form and use that is being retained and inherited within the enclosure system.

45% of land parcels defined as consisting of quickset hedges were located in the 'survey-planned' historic landscape character stratum. In contrast only 17% of quickset hedges are found within the earlier 'retentive' stratum of historic landscape character. This supports the idea that much of the 'survey-planned' areas represent a reorganisation of the landscape probably since the post-medieval period that has resulted in the geometric, straight edged fields that formed part of the agricultural improvement of that age.

This rapid study shows the potential of trying to understand the historical development of the landscape assisted by the study of the nature and distribution of trees within it. Rather than trying to date individual hedgerows through the contentious study of counting tree species over a set distance (Muir, 2000) this study offers a method for the rapid appraisal of the form of tree cover that actually exists now, but with a clear historical reference.

9.5 Local distinctiveness: Buildings

One of the most obvious features of any landscape and its history is the type of built heritage that exists within an area. There is an interest in old buildings and preserving them for their architectural merits or for being diagnostic of local building tradition. This results in the 'listing' and grading of buildings in an area. One approach to investigating the contribution of the built heritage to an area would therefore be to study the Listed Buildings recorded within the Arrow Valley.

However studying Listed Buildings would only include by the very nature of the listings the more elaborate or unique buildings of an area rather than provide an overview of the general trend in building style. Therefore, how can the character of buildings be registered? One albeit fairly crude measure is the documenting of the building materials used in its construction or subsequent maintenance or alteration.

As part of the Arrow Valley project this study was undertaken for as many of the buildings that could be recorded within the time as part of the field survey work undertaken by the project team. The main form of construction of each building was recorded (for instance timber framed or brick) and the roof material. For timber framed buildings further detail was obtained recording its treatment, whether it consisted of wattle and daub, brick infill or weather boarding. The current usage and previous usage was recorded where it was possible to define

for example a barn conversion or former rural industry (eg 'The Old Forge').

The overall total of buildings recorded was 837 and we estimate that this represents approximately 30% of the total number of buildings in the Arrow Valley. A feature of this sample is that the coverage of buildings recorded is not consistent across the entire valley. Good coverage of buildings recorded was achieved across Staunton, Pembridge, south Lyonshall and southern Leominster and Monkland parishes while the parishes of Kington and Huntington and Titley are, in comparison, under represented with limited recording of the built heritage.

Eardisland parish is well represented although this may be because the village of Eardisland was surveyed completely. The buildings surrounding the village were not recorded except for the southern area of Eardisland parish and into southern Pembridge parish. The larger urban areas of Kington and Leominster were not included in the survey as emphasis was upon the rural landscape. Other significant settlements were recorded such as Staunton-On-Arrow and the hamlets of Marston,

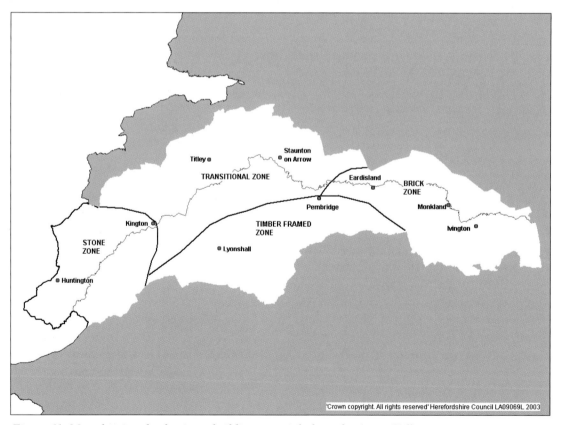

Figure 61 Map showing the dominant building material along the Arrow Valley

Rhyse, Lewis Wych, Bearwood, Lower Bearwood, Holme Marsh, Lower Broxwood, Weston and Ivington.

A general overview of the type of building material can be obtained by analysing the data, bearing in mind the limitations of the sample. Brick buildings were the most frequently occurring within the sample at 39.9% followed by timber framed buildings at 27.5% and then stone at 16.9%. This figure may not be an accurate reflection of the entire built heritage due to the gaps in the survey data, in particular the Huntington and Kington area, which are dominated by stone buildings. This area only formed 3.6% of the total number of buildings surveyed. On the other hand, the south Leominster and Monkland areas were surveyed to a greater degree (27.2% of the total number of buildings surveyed) and in this area it is clear that brick buildings predominate. Even so, an appraisal of the form of buildings along the river valley can be attempted.

At the western extent of the Arrow Valley, around Kington and Huntington 60% of the buildings were constructed of stone, with 38.5% of the Titley and north Lyonshall area also characterised by stone buildings. Although present, timber framed buildings were not common or recorded in the same number as the stone buildings within the area. In contrast, at the eastern extent of the valley a different picture can be seen. In Leominster and Monkland, 60% of the buildings are brick, followed by timber framed buildings (16.2%) of the buildings surveyed within this area. 45.5% of Eardisland and the south east Pembridge area is dominated by brick buildings with a third of all buildings within this area recorded as timber framed.

In the central reaches of the Arrow Valley there is a further contrast to the building traditions recorded at either end of the valley. Along the southern edge of the study area (southern Lyonshall, Kington Rural and Pembridge) the buildings are dominated by timber framing (42%). This is followed by brick at 28.8% then stone at only 10.5%. However the northern area of the Arrow Valley, from the east of Titley through to Shobdon and along the River Arrow to north Lyonshall and Pembridge, features the least variation between the main categories in the use of building materials. Timber framing was

the most common (29.5%) followed closely by stone buildings at (25.9%) and brick at (24.7%).

Within the valley, there were other forms to the framework and treatment of buildings. For instance, 9% of the total number of buildings were steel frame constructions used in modern agricultural buildings. This illustrates the need by farmers and landowners to replace earlier buildings and the extent to which the rural economy manifests itself within the landscape through the built environment. In the Titley and northern Lyonshall area 16.5% of buildings recorded were steel framed while around Eardisland the same percentage of stone buildings were recorded as with steel framed buildings (8%). A problem encountered by the survey teams was the number of rendered buildings (nearly 10% of the total number of buildings recorded) that made it difficult, if not impossible, to assess the original framework and materials used in the construction of the building.

Of the 214 timber framed buildings surveyed 38% have slate roofs, 27% have clay tiles and 25% have corrugated iron roofs. This high percentage of corrugated iron initially surprised the surveyors but when the majority of timber framed buildings within the area are agricultural buildings it is clear that this roofing material is a cheaper and efficient way of roofing old barns that may have been originally thatched, for instance. Timber framed buildings also showed the greatest variation in treatment of the walls. Many of the domestic dwellings especially in the southern area of the Arrow Valley are derived from a small timber framed cottage, where the wattle and daub has been removed and brick has been used to infill the gaps. Approximately only 13% of timber framed buildings that were recorded retain walls consisting of wattle and daub, while 17% contains brick infill. However 30% of timber framed buildings have timber weather boarding and this was observed, in varying states of repair, on recent barn conversions and retained agricultural barns.

From this limited survey of the buildings of the Arrow Valley it is clear that there are distinct trends within the landscape that relate to the use of different building materials. In the western part of the valley the construction of buildings is dominated by stone, while downstream on the southern side of the valley buildings are characterised by timber

Figure 62 Enlargement of an aerial photograph of Lower Hengoed near Huntington showing the impact of new building construction upon the traditional farm complex. ©HAAS 03-CN- 1702

framing. In the central northern area of the valley there appears to be a 'transitional' zone where the three main construction types are present in roughly equal numbers. In the lower reaches of the river the buildings are characterised by brick (Figure 61). This study has shown that the image of a landscape dominated by timber framed or 'black-and-white' houses is false. This form of building is limited to one area of the valley within which it provides the local character of the building stock. The survey has provided a unique insight into the character of the area by investigating part of the historic environment that is often overlooked.

9.6 Local distinctiveness: Farm complexes

A neglected aspect of the local distinctiveness of the rural landscape is the nature of the agricultural buildings now present. It was realised in the development of this project from initial ideas, that a study of farm complexes could give an indication of the rate of change of the built component of the rural landscape. A farm complex is defined here as

the core buildings around the main farmhouse or residence (or former such focus of a farm holding). The 1964, 1983 and most recent Ordnance Survey maps were studied and the increase or decrease in the number and scale of buildings was noted (Figure 62).

Between 1964 and 1983 the size of most farm complexes remained fairly static. There are indications that new buildings have been constructed within or adjacent to farm complexes, but these appear to replace older buildings and the new buildings are situated on the existing foundations with what appears to be a limited increase in area. Many of these buildings are related to those farms that have had or continue to have a sizeable animal stock on the farm holding and that therefore require adequate accommodation for the animals. This was confirmed through the farm surveys and interviews with the farmers. From the 1960s onwards, many of the older timber framed buildings were no longer in a suitable state of repair or could not accommodate the newer and larger agricultural machinery. As a result these buildings

Figure 63 An example of the increasing number of 'off-farm' complexes that are appearing in the landscape of the Arrow Valley

were replaced while the overall size of the farm complexes along the Arrow Valley remained the same.

Between 1983 and today there has been a considerable change in the structure of the farm complexes however. The erection of large sheds on farm complexes has had the effect of expanding the historic core of the farm between half again of its original size to over triple the original size. One trend has involved the construction of newer barns and cattlesheds. This did happen previously, but now the earlier buildings are being retained and used for storage, or are converted into residential dwellings.

Since 1983 another impact on the historic landscape has been an increase in the number of off- farm buildings being constructed. These are buildings sited away from the traditional farm complexes often in what could be considered open countryside.

An example of this sort of building is the poultry house complexes that have been established since the early 1980s and are still being built to the present day. There were poultry houses at Nextend, Lewis Wych and Lower House near Ivington before 1983. Since then there have been increases in these complexes within the Arrow Valley, especially around the Lyonshall area, the newest having been built in 2002/3.

This study shows that there are definite trends within this in the development of farm buildings. The review of the farm complexes was based upon a map analysis of the buildings rather than a visual study of the buildings. Although the footprint of a building may have remained the same, technological developments in construction techniques have allowed higher buildings to be built with the roofline being raised in the landscape. This may have an impact upon the character not only of the historic farm complex itself but also of the surrounding countryside.

The effect of off-farm industurial- scale units can be dramatic in a topographically- diverse landscape such as that of the Arrow Valley (Figure 63). In some cases, considerable efforts have been made, no doubt as a requirement of planning permission, to tuck poultry units into hillsides to minimise their visual impact. An example is the complex at The Heath Farm, Lyonshall. Unfortunately the impact of the complex built in 2002/3 south of Lynhales has not been softened in this way.

Parish	Surveyed Land Parcels	Unsurveyed Land Parcels	Parish Totals	% Surveyed
Huntington	81	271	352	23.01
Kington	30	99	129	23.26
Kington Rural	181	949	1,130	16.02
Titley	52	161	213	24.41
Lyonshall	182	282	464	39.22
Pembridge	402	369	771	52.14
Staunton-on-Arrow	126	123	249	51.21
Eardisland	49	371	420	11.67
Monkland and Stretford	36	101	137	26.28
Leominster	253	234	487	51.95
Totals	1,392	2960	4,352	31.98

Table 5 The number of land parcels per parish recorded as part of the Arrow Valley project

9.7 Agricultural processes

As part of the Arrow Valley project a sample survey of land use was undertaken on the ground on a field-by-field basis. This required visiting and recording as much of the Arrow Valley farmland as was possible within the project time parameters. Although the survey was not completed for the entire valley in as far as that not every single land parcel (field) was recorded, a third of the river valley was surveyed and each parish had a proportion of its fields recorded. This varied from an over 50% sample for quarter of the parishes to only 12% for one of the parishes (Table 5).

The survey was undertaken by driving around the landscape and taking advantage of the natural topography and road access to try and record as much as was feasible. This reduced the time required to seek permission to access land but also accounts for a percentage of the area that was not recorded if a land parcel was not visible from a public viewpoint. The current land use was recorded within the land parcel along with other parameters such as type of slope and its declivity. We were interested to try and gauge the extent of landscape change since World War II and the possible rate of erosion in terms of increased runoff from ploughing upon slopes or the need to drain low-lying or wet fields. These processes may have an impact upon buried archaeological deposits. This data was entered onto a Geographical Information System (GIS) layer and could be cross-referenced and analysed with other data.

One recorded characteristic was the distribution of potato cultivation within the Arrow Valley. Nearly 68% of these fields were located on a steep or moderate slope, which may have an impact of increased soil erosion. 76% of the potato production recorded within the survey was located at the top or on the upper to mid slopes of the valley where soils are at their thinnest. This may be having a severe impact upon the sub-stratum of soils in these locations.

Through the use of a GIS it was possible to cross reference the data from the field survey with an earlier land use map, that of Dudley Stamp's *Land Utilisation Map* of Britain dating to the inter-War period undertaken by the London School of Economics. Table 6 shows that the amount of arable

Stamp/Today	Arable	Grassland	Orchard
Arable	49%	39%	8%
Grass	27%	59%	3%
Orchard	18%	45%	21%

Table 6 Comparison of land use change between Stamp's map and the survey data collected as part of the Arrow Valley project

	Stamp	Today
Arable	12%	30%
Grassland	76%	54%
Orchard	6%	4%
Woodland	3%	6%

Table 7 Percentage change in land use between Stamp and today per recorded land parcel in the Arrow Valley

cultivation has increased by 18% within the surveyed area of the Arrow Valley with the amount of grassland declining by 22%. What is interesting to note is that the amount of orchard has declined while the number of land parcels of woodland has increased. The decrease in orchards may actually be accounted for by the loss of orchards around farm buildings where cider was produced for personal consumption and the trees have been subsequently removed. Meanwhile the cider industry is now organised on an industrial scale. The increase in woodland may reflect the recent trend to provide landowners with funding to plant areas of woodland on the least agriculturally productive areas of land.

Further analysis of the land use changes revealed that nearly half of the land parcels that were arable on the Stamp map were still arable while 27% of the grassland has changed to arable. Around the Weston and Staunton areas arable land has been converted to orchards but the general trend in the loss of orchards is revealed in Table 7 where 45% of orchards upon the Stamp map have converted to grassland and 18% to arable.

Changes in the agriculture regimes can ultimately have an impact on the archaeology and historic environment of an area. The increase of arable cultivation has the effect of increasing the rate of erosion of soils and subsoils especially on hillslopes. The effect of ploughing on a slope is the transportation of soil downslope which results in the depth of any buried archaeological deposits located on the top of a slope or on the slope becoming closer to the plough which results in the damage and deplacement of artefacts and buried deposits. Ploughing also results in the erosion of earthworks that can be observed especially within pasture fields.

Earthworks survive also in traditional orchards, so it can be assumed that earthwork loss has been considerable. In contrast industrial orcharding is preceded by bulldozing to level the ground and extensive groundworks particularly for drainage and this can also have a substantial impact upon an earthworks or buried archaeology.

Chapter summary: some key points

- The work described in this chapter constitutes a first attempt in Herefordshire (but also more generally) to identify indicators of historic landscape change through landscape-wide analysis.

- Change in the landscape can be registered by boundary loss, but boundary change is a more subtle and complex process.

- A general trend in the Arrow Valley has been the removal of boundaries that once defined plocks or small enclosures, especially near settlements.

- The greatest changes in the rural built environment have been in the height of barns and similar facilities around farmyards, and the creation of off-farm intensive rearing units.

- Study of trees especially in hedgerows has emphasised the longevity of boundaries even where the landscape may have been re-organised in the past 300 years.

- The increase in arable and loss of traditional orchards is likely to have had a marked impact on the historic environment - in terms of loss of visible earthworks and the erosion of buried archaeological features.

PART FOUR

CONSERVATION

Chapter 10

The care and management of ancient monuments

10.1 Introduction

This last part of the report explores the question of the conservation of the historic monuments within the Arrow Valley. Monuments – by which is meant here highly visible earthworks from the past - make a substantial contribution to our sense of cultural and historical identity and continuity. Ancient monuments are integral parts of our modern environment and are not just fossilised elements of a static historic landscape (Bapty, 2000). They often mark out what is most distinctive about a particular area or region.

One aspect of conservation is the protection of monuments from active erosion and the need to maintain these monuments, in a practical way, for future generations. A key objective of the Arrow Valley project was to undertake practical conservation works upon one or more such monuments. The aim was also however to raise awareness for the need for appropriate management of this kind, and to convey the message that this need not be an expensive way to enhance a monument.

This chapter explores what monuments exist within the Arrow Valley and how they can be best managed. The reasons why some archaeological features (and not others) are protected by legislation are explained. The most frequent impacts upon historical monuments are specified here, while examples are provided of positive management actions with reference to a couple of sites within the Arrow Valley.

10.2 Monuments in the landscape: designation and protection

Within the totality of surviving archaeological traces in the landscape, there are those monuments that are exceptional for their scale, rarity, group value or degree of preservation. These are the foremost monuments that are considered important to be conserved for future generations. Such monuments are mostly designated as Scheduled Ancient Monuments (SAMs). There are twenty such SAMs within the Arrow Valley study area.

As noted in Chapter 2, this total includes six intermittent sections of Offa's Dyke, five motte and bailey castles, four undated mounds of varying size and description, three prehistoric barrows, two hillforts, one moated site and a linear dyke system (Rowe Ditch) that traverses the river valley near Pembridge. As previously noted, these monuments represent a small percentage of the known archaeology within the Arrow Valley. In fact, even if the intermittent sections of Offa's Dyke are considered as separate monuments, the SAMs represent less than 4% of the total SMR figure. These archaeological monuments represent a diverse group of sites ranging from prehistoric times to the medieval period. But how and why are they protected?

Although the desire to protect ancient features is long-standing the concern to protect them under statute originated in the late 19th century. Celebrated cases such as the destruction of Devil's Dyke in Oxfordshire were recorded in Parliament. This led to the first Ancient Monuments Act in 1882. The most recent reformulation of this legislation is the Ancients Monuments and Archaeological Areas Act, 1979. The act of 'Scheduling' a site does not necessarily mean that it is under immediate threat from destruction. Rather, it designates that site as being of national importance. As such it is legally protected for future generations to enjoy as we do today (English Heritage, 1999). A list of potentially

Figure 64 The motte at Staunton-on-Arrow from the southeast, taken in 2000 before the scrub clearance and site managment works. ©WNFC/ MASH 00-C-0378

damaging works has been specified in the Act, providing circumstances under which the consent of the relevant Secretary of State must be gained before the commencement of those works. English Heritage provide guidance to the minister concerned as to whether such works are allowable, and with what conditions attached to the consent. The procedures were further formalised in the National Heritage Act, 1984.

10.3 Monuments in the landscape: monitoring and management

The form of the ancient monuments that we see in the landscape today is the result of centuries of weathering and the slow process of erosion. For instance the ditches and ramparts of the Iron Age hillforts are shaped by erosion by long term weathering. The ditches have become filled in while the ramparts have become rounded. We therefore only see today part of the original profile of the defences and scale of the construction of the hillfort. This suggests that the level of survival, form and composition of archaeological monuments will affect their continued survival (Rimmington, 2000).

It could be argued that over a very long time the bank and ditch would return to a flat level area. There is a natural decay to the monument. Experiments have shown, however, that earthworks stabilise after initial weathering. The effect of natural erosion is then almost imperceptible and it is other aspects of erosion such as animal burrowing that have a larger impact and therefore need to be taken into account (Bapty, 2000). It is where the erosion is accelerated that particular concern should be raised.

This can involve a series of factors from the growth of undergrowth and sapling trees upon the monument to damage such as animal burrowing or intensive grazing of animals. Humans can also have a direct impact on the survival of a monument through rutting caused by machinery, the construction of accessways or by subsoiling and drainage works.

For Scheduled Ancient Monuments, there is a system in place for the routine monitoring of the condition of a monument. This is carried out by Field Monument Wardens employed by English Heritage to make regular monitoring visits. During

Figure 65 The motte at Staunton-on-Arrow from the northeast taken during the summer of 2003 showing the extent of the site management works and the better definition of the mound. ©HAAS 03-C-1260

these visits, the officers concerned make observations about any changes that have occurred since their last visit, and pass on recommendations to the regional archaeological Inspector of Ancient Monuments. The Inspector routinely advises upon applications for Scheduled Monument Consent for works affecting SAMs.

The Field Monument Wardens also seek actively to promote sound management of the monuments concerned. To this end, they meet with the landowners or tenants of the land upon which the monument stands, and they provide informal advice on for instance acceptable livestock stocking levels. Where appropriate, they will also seek to enter into management agreements concerning the overall future regime for optimal care of the monument. These are formal agreements, and may attract some limited funding. Such agreements may in turn form part of more extensive agreements, such as are put in place where agri-environment schemes are in operation.

The appropriate management of monuments is a balance between the values placed on that monument and its character. It is generally accepted

that a short permanent grass cover is the best to ensure the condition of the buried remains and to provide clarity for the visitor to the monument. It is important to recognise the other values that are placed on a monument, also.

Monuments that are not under arable cultivation but have remained visible in the landscape sometimes become a reserve not only for archaeology but also for ecology or valued for its public amenity. As such people associate the monument more with these values than the archaeology or history of the site itself.

The actual work of vegetation clearance is not necessarily a simple and straightforward matter. For instance, the presence of different wildlife species and the nature of local land management needs to be taken into account. The total removal of trees or undergrowth may be considered beneficial for the conservation of the archaeology but is not necessarily the appropriate action for the ecology at the site.

As part of monument management there are two levels of management that can be considered. The first level is critical management where work may need to be carried out to limit the damage occurring on a monument that is threatening the survival of archaeological deposits. The second level is optional management where work may be carried out that could enhance the understanding of the monument's setting or to improve access to the monument.

The issues raised so far can be explored through examples of the management on a couple of Scheduled Ancient Monuments within the Arrow Valley, at the Staunton-on-Arrow motte and Rowe Ditch.

10.4 Staunton-on Arrow motte

Quite when the medieval lordship of Stanton or Staunton was established is unknown. This castle mound is therefore a silent witness to an important stage in its development, dating back as it does to the early years of Norman dominion in the late eleventh century. An Anglo-Saxon charter describes an estate here, which was laid waste in the Welsh Wars of the 1060s. In 1086, the settlement had six household heads, and its lord was one Drogo, who held it under Osbern, the son of Richard Scrope of Richard's Castle.

The circular earthen mound, or motte, was a French innovation, and several depictions of such mounds are sewn in the Bayeux Tapestry. It was usually surmounted by a strong timber tower, which served as a refuge and lookout. The main hall and ancillary buildings were probably sited in the bailey. Here at Staunton, the main bailey to the south of the castle is still in evidence today. It terminates to the south in a massive bank, with a deep external ditch that has for many centuries been adapted as a mill leat. The Staunton motte (SAM Herefordshire 120) very much typifies the condition of some of the castle sites in Herefordshire. The undergrowth and trees at the beginning of 2003 were so prolific that the shape of the motte could not be seen. Visitors to Staunton often found it hard to believe that there was such a prominent mound next to the churchyard here. It was therefore considered critical to undertake management works upon the monument.

A photograph taken of the motte as part of the Royal Commission Survey on Historical Monuments in England (RCHME, 1934; Plate 5) shows a grass covered mound with no undergrowth. The trees that are situated on the top of the motte now were also present, albeit much smaller.

As part of the Arrow Valley project, volunteers from the community undertook some limited site management works at the motte. Following Scheduled Monument Consent from English Heritage part of the eastern and southern side of the mound was cleared of undergrowth and trees were coppiced (Figures 64 and 65). Mature trees that exist on the top of the mound have become part of the recognised landscape and have become a valued integral part of the monument itself and the wider landscape. As such these were not touched.

The retention of undergrowth on the western and northern sides helps to maintain the wildlife and ecology balance, as the motte itself is one of the few places in the county that Danewort is recorded as existing. Also maintaining some scrub will hopefully limit the movement of animals and people on and around the monument and limit the area under potential erosion by trampling. During 2003 the monument, and field it is situated in, was grazed by a limited number of sheep following the management works.

The clearance of undergrowth did reveal active damage to the monument through the burrowing of rabbits especially on the southern side of the motte. The warren holes can be clearly seen and the spoil from the burrows has started to redefine the profile of the mound resulting in a series of small terraces upon its southern slope. It is hoped that the removal of undergrowth cover preferred by rabbits, from around these holes will deter further damage from burrowing by animals in this are. This will need to be monitored further to assess the impact the rabbits are having to the integrity of the monument.

The scrub management has had a radical effect on the awareness of the monument. It has completely transformed a visitor's appreciation of the presence and significance of the castle mound at Staunton. Apart from the damage to the archaeology from tree saplings and brambles it would not be surprising that before the management work were undertaken for visitors to the church or churchyard to hardly notice that the motte was there, shrouded in dense tree cover and saplings along with undergrowth.

Aspects of monument monitoring and management were discussed at a workshop organised as part of the Arrow Valley project. This workshop addressed the role of English Heritage in scheduling sites, how the area of the monument is defined within the schedule and the need for consent to undertake any works.

Issues regarding ecology were addressed with arguments for and against the total removal of undergrowth and tree cover. Concern was expressed by landowners and residents for scrub management that involved its total removal mentioning the potential impacts upon the ecology and what is believed to be the visual coherence of the landscape cover. Some of the advantages of retaining limited scrub or undergrowth upon a monument were discussed.

Reference was made to the English Heritage owned Wigmore Castle, in the north of the county, where a naturalistic approach to vegetation cover across the site is used to guide visitors around the monument as well as provide a picturesque atmosphere to the ruins. By retaining some undergrowth it is possible to produce a natural 'out of bounds' area where wildlife can survive. This creation of an 'exclusion zone' also limits access either by humans or grazing animals.

It was also noted that the removal of mature trees would be far more damaging by uprooting the trees and disturbing the buried archaeological deposits and instead the coppicing of existing trees should be promoted so that sunlight can reach the ground and improve the grass swaith upon the monument. The aim of future management on the site would be to restrict new growth of saplings as new roots would be more damaging in comparison to the established root systems of mature trees.

What the management works have achieved at Staunton-on-Arrow is the re-inscribing of the motte as a landmark. When walking up the church pathway the motte dominates the area to the west beyond the churchyard wall. The grass slopes of the mound provide an indication of the proximity of the monuments to the church and to the rest of the village. The scrub management has also provided the chance to see the landscape from the motte itself. From the top of the mound, the significance of its location becomes obvious with commanding views

across the river valley to Pembridge, downstream to Eardisland and towards Kingsland situated between the Rivers Arrow and Lugg.

10.5 Rowe Ditch

The historical significance of Rowe Ditch has been described earlier in Chapter 5 but it is summarised here. Rowe Ditch remains as the most obvious feature of the early Anglo Saxon period within this part of the county. Its orientation and form suggest a defensive structure and it seems that it probably dates from the earliest arrival of the English in numbers in the Arrow Valley, c. AD 650. The line of the ditch and bank reflects a political division within the landscape.

There are substantial conservation issues concerning the care and maintenance of this linear historic feature. As with the motte at Staunton, Rowe Ditch is a Scheduled Ancient Monument (SAM Herefordshire 117: 'North Herefordshire Rowe Ditch') but it is subject to different conservation pressures. The very nature of the monument itself as a linear monument poses potential problems for management. For instance, along its four-kilometre (approximately two mile) length it is crossed by three roads, and its southern end becomes invisible as it approaches another road, the A44 to the west of Pembridge.

Because the monument spans the river valley, ownership along the monument changes. A potential result is a varying level of maintenance that contributes to its management. The surviving earthwork sections are sometimes isolated in the landscape due to the past removal of sections that did not provide convenient hedge lines in the farmed landscape and have subsequently been ploughed. Other sections have had the ditch on the western side of the monument filled in. The line of the monument is now marked by substantial trees and hedge line in the landscape. As with the mature trees on the Staunton-on-Arrow motte, these prominent features are valued in the landscape today.

The most considerable ongoing threat to the monument is the existence of over-mature trees actually growing on the monument that are susceptible to being blown over in strong winds (Figure 66). Equally, the establishment of new saplings will continue to damage the remaining bank material. There is therefore an ongoing need to manage the vegetation, and carry out works designed to thin out the cover and remove trees vulnerable to wind-throw. A programme of coppicing over a period of years, in a series of limited areas, would enhance the earthwork remains but would also limit the impact upon the wildlife and the landscape.

Along its line through the Leen Farm, the earthwork is fenced off on both sides. This provides not only a wildlife 'corridor' across the valley but is conserving the monument from further other erosive impacts. The hooves of cattle can be damaging to earthworks and if the monument was not fenced off, damage from cattle seeking shelter or using trees as rubbing posts would result in the rapid deterioration of the earthwork.

10.6 The condition of monuments in the Arrow Valley

It was not possible within the scope of this project to carry out a general condition survey of the protected and other earthwork monuments in the whole valley. However, it is worth pointing out some

Figure 66 Rowe Ditch is marked in the landscape by mature trees along its length

of the kinds of processes affecting several of the monuments.

The most considerable unprotected monument, but one vulnerable to land-use change, is the earthwork remains of Lyonshall medieval town, surviving in pasture to the north of the present village crossroads.

Meanwhile, in the same village, the damage that tree-throws can potentially do was illustrated by the collapse of an enormous beech-tree onto the keep of Lyonshall Castle (SAM Herefordshire 108). The tree had been growing hard up against the stump of the western wall of the keep, and the way in which

Figure 67 The wind blown tree at Lyonshall Castle. People within the photograph show the scale of the root system

the tree fell did actually minimise its destructive force – leading to a curious sight by mid-2003 (Figure 67).

The castle remains at Lyonshall are moderately extensive, with both a keep and a stone-walled inner bailey, and an outer bailey surrounded by an earthwork that might once also have featured a stone-built enclosing wall. Several lengths of the encompassing moat are also still water-filled. This site, although in a private garden and inaccessible to the public except by invitation, is nonetheless well cared for by its owners.

The most extensive medieval castle remains in the valley are nonetheless not at Lyonshall, but at Huntington (SAM Herefordshire 99). Here, it is not so much tree growth, but the uncontrolled growth of vegetation and the lack of any protection for the walls and towers of the medieval structures that is causing a general collapse of the ruins.

It was noted however within the Arrow Valley project, following liaison with a local resident and landowner that the Scheduled Ancient Monument known as 'Monk's Court', in Eardisland (SAM Herefordshire 97) is at risk of erosion from the course of the River Arrow. Located at the western end of the village the circular earthwork monument is currently only twelve metres from the course of the river. From map analysis, the riverbank at this point has eroded over two and half metres in less than a century. Despite efforts from English Heritage to limit the bank erosion by a wicker baffle, the northern bank of the river continues to encroach

into the field at a considerable rate where the baffle does not extend to along the riverbank. This has already resulted in a riverside footpath being washed away. This case demonstrates the active erosion that can occur as a result of river channel change.

Meanwhile, it is not only the remains themselves, but also the setting of at least one of the castles in the valley that has been subject to attrition. This is the motte at Eardisland (SAM Herefordshire 96), where the former district planning authority (and apparently English Heritage) allowed the construction of an estate of modern houses around the north and west of the monument, entirely compromising its setting.

On a larger scale, some monuments have been managed actively in order to increase the amenity value of a monument. In the immediate pre-Second World War period, for instance, the hillfort at Wapley Hill (SAM Herefordshire 19175) was planted up with conifers. By the late 1980s, however, the loss of visibility of the monument had been appreciated, and the Forestry Commission cleared both the defences and the interior of the Iron Age hillfort, and provided discrete interpretation panels for the monument.

Chapter summary: some key points

- This chapter has revealed the need for positive management on historical monuments. This management does not necessarily need to be costly to provide a better dividend for important sites within the landscape, for instance at Staunton-on Arrow motte.

- The site management work at Staunton-on-Arrow motte has vastly improved its appearance and has re-established it as a key feature not only within the village but in the surrounding landscape.

- The varying perceptions and values assigned to a monument, such as its wildlife and amienty value needs to be considered when undertaking management works and to respond accordingly

- Apart from new tree growth and animal damage the River Arrow itself can be an agent of destruction to the archaeological integrity of a monument

Chapter 11

The dynamics of conservation

11.1 Introduction

The previous chapter showed that monuments are not fossilised remains of a bygone age but an integral part of the current landscape. Consequently, historic monuments are dynamic in that there is an interaction of the monument with a range of processes in its surrounding environment. In this chapter, we are looking instead at the dynamics of archaeology and historic features in the wider landscape. Two elements are considered here: agri-environment schemes, and the assessment of landscape-wide trends in resource erosion.

The advent of such agri-environment schemes represents the beginning of a shift from subsidy via the quota system and grants for production, to a more management-led system. In the future, farm payments will be linked to a number of planned outputs, one of the most important being environmental gain and management. One of these schemes is Countryside Stewardship and farmers within the Arrow Valley have taken it up.

Meanwhile, we have hardly made a start in assessing patterns of loss and erosion of the archaeology and historic features within the landscape. The survival of an archaeological site is linked to not only its form and character but also to its historical management. Its discovery is inherently linked to its erosion, for instance the discovery of a cropmark site is due to the active erosion of the site by the process of ploughing. It is thereby subsequently discovered by aerial photography and recorded.

It is not possible to record every site before it is eroded away or to know the full extent of archaeological or historic features due to earlier erosion in the past, but attempts can be made to enhance our understanding of the distribution of archaeological sites in the landscape. By registering potential destruction factors against other factors such as topography and land use it may be possible to develop a risk and resource model that can inform us of where erosion has occurred or the loss of

archaeological deposits are being accelerated due to destruction factors in the landscape.

11.2 Countryside Stewardship

Countryside Stewardship is one of ten schemes that form part of the England Rural Development Programme (ERDP). Originally established as a pilot scheme by the Countryside Commission in 1991, the scheme was transferred to MAFF (now DEFRA) in 1996. Managed by DEFRA's Rural Development Service (RDS) the scheme makes payments to farmers and land managers to improve the natural beauty and diversity of the countryside. The aim is to make conservation part of land management. The scheme is voluntary and discretionary with applications invited from anyone who manages land with a secure tenure of ten or more years. DEFRA then has the discretion to select those applications which best demonstrate the objectives of the scheme (Jago, 1995; Berry, 2000).

This includes the retention of historic landscapes such as parks and unimproved pasture as well as restoring elements of the historic and traditional landscapes such as the restoration of standard (traditional) orchards or the maintenance of hedgerows and field boundaries. The aim of Countryside Stewardship is to promote best practice in agricultural methods. The scheme seeks to restore and then to maintain areas that have become degraded. Through a series of works, the farmer can sign up to a ten-year agreement that can be renewed thereafter.

Clearly, the emphasis has been upon the natural environment rather than the historic environment within the Stewardship schemes. However there can still be an inherent interest in the good management of farmland for ecological reasons, the effect of which can have a practical benefit to the management of historical monuments.

There are approximately thirty farms in the Arrow Valley signed up to a Countryside Stewardship agreement (M. Williams, FWAG, pers. comm.). Many of the schemes are based upon land holdings along the course of the river and it is hoped that Stewardship will protect watercourses and the surrounding landscape. As indicated in chapter 8 much of this land will be under pasture that may contain earthworks not only of historic interest but former river channels and evidence of dynamic river channel change that contains important information on the past environment.

There are indeed examples from within the Arrow Valley where Stewardship agreements have seen the preservation and management of historical monuments. These range from Scheduled Ancient Monuments such as castles to unscheduled monuments to smaller but no less important features associated with water management along the course of the river and its tributaries. Many of the agreements provide payment to retain grassland and therefore any buried or upstanding archaeological sites that may be located in the grassland.

By making visits to farms and providing advice to farmers on the potential management of the historic environment, we have become aware that traditional standard orchards can retain earthwork features. One such example was the recording of former water management features in an orchard within Pembridge parish. These were discovered during a visit in 2001 to a farmholding that was applying for Countryside Stewardship. As a result the

stewardship agreement will protect the historical earthworks under a traditional orchard management scheme. Other water management features such as leats, mill races and water meadows are also protected and enhanced with assistance from Countryside Stewardship at seven holdings along the Arrow Valley (Figure 68).

In 2000, the County Archaeologist contributed to a training event for RDS staff at one of the farms in the Staunton-on-Arrow area, and identified earthworks and former water management features.

One element of the Countryside Stewardship scheme is the repair and management of hedgerows and many agreements have involved the restoration of ancient field boundaries. This includes 'gapping up' holes within hedges and laying hedges where possible for wildlife. Apart from the wildlife benefits, the restoration of hedgerows actually retains the wider significance of the historic enclosure of the landscape. The Countryside Stewardship schemes are therefore a dynamic factor within the modern landscape in terms of conservation.

Figure 68 Earthworks such as this leat of a water meadow system between Ivingtonbury and Broadward can be preserved by Countryside Stewardship

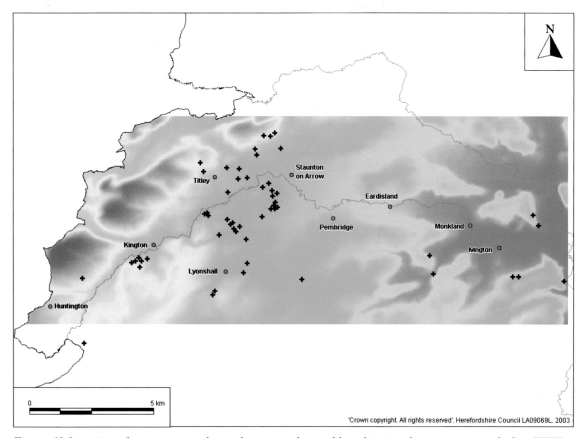

Figure 69 Location of steep convex slopes that are under arable cultivation but were pasture before WWII

An aspect of Countryside Stewardship that may not have been appreciated yet is the cumulative impact schemes may have had upon the character of the landscape in some instances. In some areas of Herefordshire, there has been a net gain in the number of hedgerows, because of Countryside Stewardship. While it is impossible to recreate a hedge that may have existed at a particular location, based upon historical map evidence there are instances of new hedges being planted to accommodate the changing management upon farms. This has seen a redefinition of the landscape enclosure and demonstrates the constantly changing nature of the landscape and the varied reasons for change.

At the time of writing, the various ERDP schemes are being assessed and a new Stewardship Scheme is being proposed to begin in 2005. This will be based on an entry level to which all farmers can potentially subscribe. Payments will vary according to the level of works or management agreements entered into.

11.3 Assessing trends in resource erosion

Beyond trying to understand the various causes of change upon monuments, the AVALCCP attempted to understand the wider trends of erosion within the landscape and the potential impact it might have upon the archaeological resource. It has already been noted that specific erosion processes can effect the condition of monuments such as burrowing animals, mechanical impacts or poaching of ground by grazing animals.

This part of the project represents tentative first steps towards understanding and possibly modelling the archaeological resource in terms of its survival, erosion and loss. In Chapter 9 changes in land use between the Tithe maps of nearly 150 years ago through to Stamp's *Land Utilisation Map* of the 1930s were compared to the current day land use and the impact of such changes for the historic environment discussed. By linking this data to other parameters about the landscape such as presence of slope and its declivity, as well as land use and potential factors for erosion. This erosion includes factors such as arable cultivation, run-off, river erosion or afforstation.

Examples of high erosion rates in arable regimes on archaeological deposits have been documented as being associated with landscape parameters such as long slopes, steep slopes and areas of high relief within fields (Oxford Archaeology, 2002). Archaeological sites located at the top of slopes are very vulnerable to erosion as the covering soil erodes downslope. This movement of soil downslope leads to colluvial deposition downslope which may protect and mask archaeological sites. The occurrence of erosion on shallow slopes depends much on type of soil, drainage, compaction, crop cover and the location of field boundaries (*ibid*).

An example of this can be provided in the Arrow Valley. Approximately one- fifth of the total land parcels surveyed were located on a slope under an arable regime. Of these land parcels 25% of slopes were characterised as having a steep declivity and suggests a potential high level of erosion. In addition, the profile of the slope also needs to be taken into consideration because this can also effect the rate and depth of erosion. For instance, it is believed that an archaeological site situated on a convex slope is at a greater risk of erosion than a site located on a straight slope.

Within the land parcels under arable cultivation and situated on a steep slope 35% of these were located on a convex slope. There is a concentration of these particular attributes in the area between Titley, Staunton-on-Arrow and Lyonshall. Other land parcels are also documented as containing similar characteristics to the south of Ivington village on the slopes below Ivington Camp and along the river channel to the south and west of Kington. When this is correlated with the former land use recorded by Stamp, nearly 75% of these are land parcels that were formerly grassland (Figure 69). This suggests that in certain areas of the valley there is an accelerated and higher risk of erosion to any archaeological sites.

This 'risk' data was then cross- referenced to existing Sites and Monuments Record. This revealed that archaeological sites are located within these land parcels and include at least seven cropmark sites across the valley. Three areas of

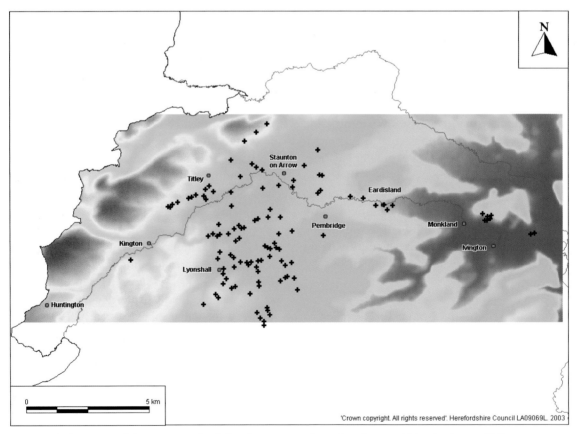

Figure 70 Location of drainage works defined as potential erosion factor within the Arrow Valley

earthworks to the north of Titley are recorded and are probably associated with former land management such as lynchets and former boundaries and around Ivington fragments of Romano- British pottery and worked flint have been recorded.

The form of the recorded site (whether a cropmark, earthwork or finds scatter) can inform us of its integrity as a site. An earthwork will be at considerable risk from being ploughed, while a wide spread of artefacts within a field would suggest that erosion had been occurring for some time resulting in the destruction of archaeological deposits and the associated artefacts being brought into the plough- zone. Similarly, a cropmark tells us also that erosion due to ploughing is responsible for the discovery of the site.

Even so, this would suggest that all of these documented sites are under active erosion that will result in their loss. What this information also highlights are the potential areas in the landscape where archaeological fieldwork could be carried out. By undertaking fieldwalking or aerial survey previously unknown sites could be revealed through targeted fieldwork that is related to the dynamics of the archaeology and its immediate environment. It should be noted that archaeological sites situated at the base of steeper slopes could actually be protected by the gradual burial of the site underneath colluvium which will create a buffer- zone between the site and the plough.

Arable is not the only threat to archaeological sites. From the survey under 4% of the land was recorded as being under threat from afforestation. There are three distinct clusters within the valley, especially to the west of Kington around Hergest, in the southern area of Pembridge parish between Lower Broxwood and Bearwood and on the valley floor near to Broadward. The majority of the afforestation has occurred on the mid valley profile of the valley and suggests slopes that may have been previously under cultivation or pasture have been converted to woodland. The intensity often associated with forest planting can result in the damaging of earthworks and buried archaeology. The plantation on the valley floor may have potential implications for the local water table and for any waterlogged environmental deposits below ground.

A further 8% of all surveyed land parcels were defined as having a threat of destruction from drainage works (Figure 70). It is not surprising to reveal that the majority of these land parcels are located in the floor of the Arrow Valley on relatively level areas. There is a concentration of drainage works in the southern area of Lyonshall parish along the course of Curl Brook. The discovery of the Bronze Age dirk in Eardisland from the up-cast of a former drainage ditch reveals the potential destruction to archaeological deposits by ditching and drainage.

One cause of resource erosion and loss that was documented at least twice along the southern edge of the Arrow Valley was the construction of barns within fields with the spoil from the levelling of the ground being dumped into another field. This process of the construction of agricultural buildings can have an effect on two parts of the landscape, at the construction site and where excess spoil is deposited. Other examples of individual areas of erosion that were also documented was the siting of animal feeders in pasture, where the concentration of animal hooves are severely damage the ground and any potential historical features.

From the survey nearly 40% of the land parcels that were surveyed had indications of compaction and rutting caused by machinery, especially around gateways into fields. Over 50% of this sample was associated with arable cultivation and was recorded along the entire river valley. Soil compaction gives rise to several agronomic problems. It is often caused by working soil when it is too wet. This results in the compaction of the soil which then results in the soil becoming denser and the greater the depth to which compaction occurs. Rutting can occur along tramlines or in especially wet conditions. Problems may also exacerbated by activities such as wetting the soil prior to potato harvesting for instance (White, 2001). Damage of this kind to archeological sites arises in three main ways. Firstly there is the direct impact of the crushing effect of the compaction upon historical features. Secondly, soil compaction often requires remedial operations to break-up the resulting soil pans. This can then in turn affect the survival and integrity of any buried archaeological deposits. Thirdly, soil compaction can result in a reduction in the depth of the ploughsoil and can ultimately

bring buried archaeological remains to the interface
with the plough (Oxford Archaeology, 2002).

Chapter summary: some key points

- Around thiry farms in the valley have current agreements in place under the Countryside Stewardship Scheme. This represents approximately 15% of the total holdings in the Arrow Valley.

- Just under half of those schemes explicitly feature historic environment gains.

- 31% of the landscape, (1,392 out of 4,352 land units) was surveyed to specify erosion parameters.

- Of this, 25% featured slopes susceptible to resource erosion.

- In the wider landscape, more general processes of erosion and decay affect the fate of archaeological and landscape features.

- The appearance of the historic landscape is being influenced by payments to farmers via so-called 'agri-environment' schemes.

- Trends in resource erosion were gauged in this project in reference to processes of soil movement on slopes under ploughing, but also through action such as drainage works, afforestation, and soil compaction.

Chapter 12

Communication and inclusion

12.1 Introduction

An important aspect of the AVALCCP was the desire to involve the community in the project in practical ways. An important aim was also to raise awareness of the historic environment within the Arrow Valley through a varied programme of events and by achieving actual tangible results in the conservation of elements of the historic environment. The partnership with the Arrow Valley Farmers group provided a particularly good basis for involving the community in this way. Through the farm survey, it was possible for farmers and landowners to contribute their time and knowledge to the project, and in some ways, this was the foundation of participation in the project.

The events and activities programme was so organised that such participation could vary according to interest. From the start of the project in February, a programme of events including talks, guided walks, excavations and open days to the public to view the excavations was devised. A comment that was often heard during the project was that people liked the idea of different levels of involvement and this attracted people with diverse interests to become engaged within project activities. From May 2003, this involved a different event nearly every week until October. Apart from these events, another form of participation was for the residents of the Arrow Valley to tell us their views on what they considered significant about the historic environment.

The outcomes from this project include this report, as well as the production of a series of leaflets that describe various aspects of the project such as monument management and landscape change. These will be available to those who contributed to the project and can be picked up from local libraries, museums and other information points. A display panel highlighting the discoveries made during the project was designed for Kington Museum and a second smaller panel was designed to complement the conservation works undertaken at Staunton-on-Arrow motte.

12.2 About the project: a programme of events

The programme of events was designed to cater for different potential levels of involvement by the public in the project. Therefore, the physical level of involvement and exertion required could vary considerably. Those who wanted to learn archaeological techniques of survey and excavation could do so by volunteering to participate in the excavations. If people just wanted to hear talks on the history of the river valley or hear about the latest

Events	February	March	April	May	June	July	August	September	October	Totals
Walks	0	0	0	0	37	25	47	2	0	111
Talks	42	0	72	50	45	79	0	0	151	397
Excavations	0	12	6	14	0	0	21	3	0	56
Open Days	0	0	0	30	0	0	65	0	0	95
Workshops	0	0	0	0	8	0	0	0	0	8
Non-event involvement	0	0	0	0	2	0	0	0	2	4
Site Management	0	12	12	0	0	0	0	0	0	24
Farm Survey	1	3	0	0	0	6	2	0	2	14
Monthly Totals	43	27	90	94	92	104	135	5	155	**751**

Table 8 Levels of community participation within the Arrow Valley project, by month and event

Figure 71 On one of the guided historic landscape walks along the Arrow Valley at Lyonshall

discoveries, they could come along to the series of evening talks. In fact, three successive programmes of events were organised and publicised from May to October 2003. These were divided into three separate two- month event programmes (May and June, July and August, and September and October). At each event, a 'head count' of the number of people attending was taken (Table 8). In total 751 'heads' were counted; this does not necessarily mean 751 different people attended the various events. However, it does provide a raw count of the people attending and contributing to the project. By far the most popular events were the various evening talks, followed by the guided historic landscape walks and the open days to the excavations during the summer.

The guided historic landscape walks were based upon the format of the popular monthly historic landscape walks led by staff members of Herefordshire Archaeology since 1999 around various parts of the county. The purpose of the walks was to show the variety of historical features that can be observed from public rights of way. The AVALCCP walks were organised during the summer months to take advantage of the evening sunlight.

The walks were located in different areas of the river valley, at Huntington, Lyonshall, Pembridge, Monkland and Ivington. By organising the walks in differing areas, the changing character of the landscape within the river valley could be observed. From the upland area around Huntington and Lyonshall to the relatively level landscape of Monkland and Ivington various historic monuments were observed. These ranged from the obvious such as castles, a shrunken medieval village, Offa's Dyke and the old railway line to less obvious remains of earlier landscape organisation such as water meadows, ridge and furrow and the remnants of former settlement or building platforms in corners of fields (Figure 71). In August a 'Hillfort Weekend' event was organised with guided walks along public footpaths to Wapley Hillfort and to Ivington Camp hillfort. This provided an opportunity to visit these monuments and to discuss the impact of historical and modern land use upon both sites. The development of each hillfort was explained, as was the setting of the hillfort within the wider landscape.

Following the initial talks highlighting the start of the project to local residents, a series of monthly evening talks were organised. These were very successful and well supported by the community with talks organised in the various village halls or meeting rooms in the Arrow Valley. This peripatetic pattern of provision ensured that the project was featured and was accessible within each part of the river valley.

Leading specialists were invited to discuss their research and explain the interest of the Arrow Valley to their work. Professor Mark Macklin started the series of talks with a discussion about the aims and objectives of the geomorphological study along the Arrow. Mark returned in October to present the results of the work (see Chapter 6). This was then followed by talks on the history of the Arrow Valley and recent research based on a chronological order from prehistory through to the early medieval period. Speakers included Dr. Keith Ray, County Archaeologist, Dr. Peter Guest of Cardiff University, and Ian Bapty, Offa's Dyke Archaeological Management Officer. Two further talks undertaken by the author and Tim Hoverd of Herefordshire Archaeology highlighted specific elements of landscape management. These included a 'Landscape Masterclass' that explored the historic development of the landscape, and a description of the history of woodland within Herefordshire and how recent archaeological surveys are revealing a far more complex history to the landscape than hitherto suspected. The series of talks were concluded by two talks by the author on the various results of the project.

A conservation workshop was specifically organised for farmers and landowners during June to discuss management issues regarding a group of Scheduled Ancient Monuments in the Arrow Valley in an informal manner. We are grateful to Judith Leigh, English Heritage Field Monument Warden, for contributing her time, expertise and experience to this event. Staunton-on-Arrow motte, Rowe Ditch and the Court House Moat in Pembridge were visited. The purpose of scheduling ancient monuments was discussed and a brief history of each of the sites was given. Although the monuments are located in relatively close proximity to each other, the setting of each site varies considerably as do the conservation issues upon each of the monuments and this too was discussed.

Figure 72 The view from the top of the undergrowth cleared motte at Staunton, looking east towards Shobdon

The workshop also provided people with the opportunity to describe how they remember the monument appearing in the recent (and sometimes not so recent) past. For instance at Staunton-on-Arrow motte a local resident remembers as a child the ditch of the motte being more prominent especially on the north- eastern side of the mound. In fact, the base of the ditch was waterlogged during the winter months over twenty years ago and one would have had to jump across the water filled ditch to get to the mound (Figure 72).

For each of the excavations, an open day was held at the end of each week of site investigations so that visitors could see the discoveries and observe the progress made at each of the sites under investigation. Apart from revealing important archaeological finds and promoting a better understanding of the ancient history of the river valley (see Part Two of this report) these events raised awareness of the impact agriculture has upon the buried archaeology. Apart from the area around the former river channel at The Grove site, which was relatively deeply buried all the archaeological deposits were within the first 30 cms of the soil and at the interface of the depth of ploughing. This raised awareness of the gradual erosion of sites due to ploughing within the wider landscape. At the Middle Field site at The Leen, the excavation provided an answer to why one area of the field becomes water logged and compacted. This is due to a drape of clay overlying the gravel, which was deposited after the last Ice Age.

One of the especially successful events was the 'finds roadshow' where residents of the Arrow Valley were invited to bring objects they had found whether by digging in the back garden, metal detecting or during the ploughing of fields. Objects brought along included a finely made flint arrowhead from the Bearwood area of Pembridge parish, and numerous worked flint artefacts, blades and scrapers, from The Leen Farm. Pottery dating from the Late Iron Age to the post- medieval period was identified from various locations within the Arrow Valley.

One of the most interesting discoveries was the retrieval of fragments of Romano- British pottery from the gardens of Staunton-on-Arrow along with Roman coins. This suggests the possibility of a more substantial Romano- British site on the hill slope

around the church and motte at Staunton than has been previously anticipated. This information would not have become known without the programme of events that involved members of the public with the investigation of the Arrow Valley landscape and we are grateful to all those who participated.

12.3 Your views matter: a survey of attitudes

The 'historic environment' at one level is simply the area in which we live. It may also be a place of livelihood, of enjoyment, of memories and of value (English Heritage, 2000). Every generation has made its mark and each makes decisions about the future of the environment that it has inherited. In Chapter 9 elements and related issues to what contributes to the local distinctiveness of the Arrow Valley was raised. It was considered important to find out what local residents think about the historic environment and to gauge the level to which the community considers various elements of the historic environment.

A simple questionnaire was compiled to determine whether people considered the historic environment to be important to them and what historical features they felt were significant to maintain and protect for the future. Had it been possible, an attempt would have been made to follow up the results with a more detailed questionnaire that could investigate perceptions or even conduct limited interviews. However, due to the time limit this was not possible.

A total of 120 questionnaires were distributed and the sample included those people on the mailing list for the events programme. Questionnaires were also left in Leominster and Kington library to be completed and a small number of questionnaires were sent directly to residents selected at random from the local telephone directory. This questionnaire could be related to the recent 'Power of Place' report produced by English Heritage (*ibid*) that contained a MORI poll of people's opinion on the historic environment.

Approximately 42% of the Arrow Valley questionnaires were returned by the requested deadline. This means that the results can be regarded as statistically significant. From the returned questionnaires, 60% of the respondents were involved in farming or land management. The majority of the replies came from people who have lived in the Arrow Valley for more than 25 years but there was an even distribution between those who have lived here for less than 10 years and those who have lived here for up to 25 years. Some 40% of the returns came from people aged between 51 and 65, with the second largest group (26%) aged between 31 and 50 years old. Only one of the respondents was under 30 years old and this perhaps demonstrates the problem of involving this age group in community projects.

All of the completed questionnaires considered the historic environment to be important to them and moreover 66% considered it *very important* to preserve aspects of the historic environment. All those who returned the questionnaire believed that it was important to protect the buildings that are typical of an area, while 12% considered ancient footpaths, trackways and holloways not important to respect as part of the historic environment. This perhaps reflects a general unwillingness to promote better public access to the countryside - an important factor that is needed to be considered in reference to future grant- led conservation management. However 68% believe it is very important to care for trees, hedges, banks and ditches as part of the present day scene.

Although 61% believed that it was important to maintain and enhance historical sites such as churches, castles and ancient monuments as places that we may visit, several people expressed reservations about spending more money on

heritage as an investment for tourism. Only 38% believed that money should very much be invested in heritage for tourism. A comment that was made in several questionnaire returns was that tourism could ruin an area by what can be considered as the over- promotion of tourism.

One of the questions asked people to rank what feature of the historic environment they considered most and what they thought least important (Figure 73). The majority of those who returned the questionnaire thought that the landscape was the most important feature of the historic environment. Buildings and archaeological sites followed this respectively.

This survey has revealed a marked degree of respect among the residents of the Arrow Valley for the wider historic character of the landscape and its conservation. From the questionnaire results it is the visible traits of the historic environment, for instance buildings and hedges that people feel most strongly about. This is hardly surprising as it is these elements that are the most tangible references to the past. Even so, the questionnaire also revealed an interest in maintaining archaeological sites and monuments among most of those who responded.

12.4 Information on site: Staunton-on-Arrow motte

In addition to the practical scrub management of the Staunton-on-Arrow motte, it was considered

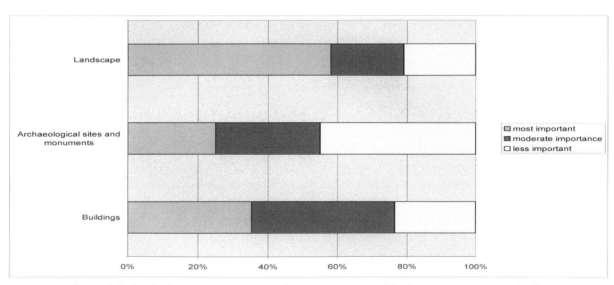

Figure 73 Chart of the level of importance given to three components of the historic environment by the respondants to the questionnaire

important to try and raise awareness of the significance of the site beyond the lifetime of this project. One way to achieve this is the erection of an information panel about the monument. The panel will complement the work that has been carried out and will provide the visitor to the Staunton-on-Arrow motte with a description of the site and a better understanding of its location. This is another reason why the maintenance work itself was important.

Given the sensitivity shown during the clearance works, it is especially important to be sensitive about the size and location of any intrusive panel. It would not be appropriate to 'clutter' the site by producing a large noticeboard or to site the panel in a location that may be detrimental to the monument.

The panel provides a brief background to the wider Arrow Valley project with an explanation of the location of the village of Staunton-on-Arrow to the surrounding landscape. This is followed by a description of the castle site itself including the construction and its subsequent management that has probably involved the location of the millrace on one side of the ditched bailey that may have enclosed the motte during the medieval period.

The panel will be in place following the necessary conditions and consents regarding its siting to the scheduled monument have been meet. The panel will also serve as a reminder of when this conservation led management of the site took place. A second panel is planned to be unveiled at Kington Museum and visitors or residents of Herefordshire can find out more about the history of this part of the county in an accessible location.

12.5 Information in the hand: leaflets

The events programme and various works carried out have succeeded in raising awareness of the need to manage the historic environment. However, it was considered important that the education and information about the results of the project extended beyond that of the lifetime of the project. As a result a small series of colour leaflets were produced as part of the conservation aim of the project.

The purpose of the leaflets is to present in a lively and accessible form the results of the project. It is hoped that the production of these leaflets will also maintain the level of interest beyond the end of the project and perhaps introduce more people to the archaeology, landscape change and conservation of the Arrow Valley. The leaflets cover the three broad topics of Monuments, Landscape Change and Conservation issues with three leaflets within each topic creating a set of nine leaflets.

Based upon an A4 folded sheet the Monuments leaflets provide an outline history of Rowe Ditch and Staunton-on-Arrow motte while the third documents the existence and purpose of leats and drainage along the river valley. The Landscape Change leaflets provide a brief description of the results of the geomorphological study, the earliest organised landscapes and the impact of agricultural improvement and reorganisation of the landscape during the post- medieval period. The Conservation leaflets cover the management of monuments, historic landscapes and water management features.

12.6 Personal action: volunteering in the Arrow Project

The overall success of the project as indicated above relied to a considerable degree upon the active involvement of the community. Although there was a high level of interest in the project shown by the number of people who came along to the talks, walks and open days, an important part of the project was the 'in-kind' contribution made by the local community. Members of the public gave their own time to the project by assisting the completion of the various outputs. In total over 950hours were contributed by members of the community by donating their time to the various activities within the project.

Farmers and landowners generously gave their time to join an archaeologist to walk over their landholding and describe some of the landscape changes that they knew about as part of the whole farm surveys. We are grateful to all the farmers and landowners who took part in this part of the project. All showed a particular interest in one or more aspects of the history of the farm or landholding and some could reveal the results of their own historical research to the survey team through

Figure 74   Staunton-on-Arrow motte, September 2003

historical maps and documents pertaining to the holding. Interest in the historic environment is seen by many of the farmers as a complementary interest to that of preserving the natural environment.

Active involvement with the project was encouraged also by giving people the opportunity to volunteer and to participate in the archaeological excavations. Participants included young (post- 16-year-old) college students interested in finding out more about a possible career in archaeology or historical research. Three local university students currently reading for an archaeology degree joined the project team at various stages over the summer months and assisted in the various fieldwork. The project provided the chance to work with professional archaeologists and gain experience while still studying.

The fieldwork also provided the opportunity for members of existing groups to take part. An example was members of the Eardisland Oral History Group at the investigations at Admarsh, Eardisland. Some other members of the community participated, who had previously volunteered to work on excavations

directed by Herefordshire Archaeology staff. They have an interest in the local history and archaeology of the area and the county and feel that through their contribution they are learning new skills, learning about the history of the area. They also simply enjoy being outdoors in the landscape. The project also introduced those with an interest in archaeology, but who are not members of a history society or group or excavated before, to participate in the excavations ranging from a day to over a week. Again, a curiosity in finding out more about local history and the opportunity to get involved in the research of the river valley at a community level was the attraction for all the volunteers. The experience of excavating and potentially finding something that may not have been seen or touched for hundreds of years is an exciting experience. Further support was also given by members of the public helping with the inputting of information onto computer.

The scrub management works at Staunton-on-Arrow motte gave members of the local community and especially several residents of Staunton-on-Arrow itself the chance to contribute to managing and maintaining the historic monuments within the village. The recent millennium book published by the community of Staunton-on-Arrow represents interest in the history of the village and parish. The potential importance of the castle site during history and the need to manage the remains better was also realised. The works allowed people to actively care for the monument by assisting the owner in its management (Figure 74).

One of the aims of the project was to raise awareness of the rural historic environment and the ancient history that manifests itself in the landscape today in its varied forms. The Arrow Valley Archaeology, Landscape Change and Conservation project has achieved this by recognising the interest within the local community that exists. By providing this community with the opportunity to get actively involved in both the investigation and maintenance of the historic environment, it has raised the profile and issues surrounding the conservation of historic monuments in the Arrow Valley.

This project could only achieve a broad overview of landscape change within the short time frame available. The project has nonetheless hopefully highlighted areas of further research not only within the Arrow Valley but also more widely in the county. The nature of erosion to archaeological remains ascribable to land use change and natural processes has been raised as part of this short project. The discoveries made during the site investigations have provided new insights into the settlement of the Herefordshire landscape and are of regional importance. The value of understanding and registering attributes of the historic environment that define the local distinctiveness of an area has been demonstrated as part of this project. This may, with further investigation in other parts of the county, provide a basis for the development of indicators of change within the rural landscape of England more generally.

This project has also shown what a valuable contribution can be made by local residents and landowners through their involvement in the work. As such, the phrase 'impossible without..' really does apply in any appraisal of the achievements of the Arrow Valley Archaeology, Landscape Change and Conservation project.

Chapter summary: some key points

- A full programme of events was organised, that included 10 talks, 8 landscape walks, 2 workshop and 5 open days for excavations.

- Although some people attended more than one event, a total of 751 attendances was logged during the period February to October.

- Conservation works and conservation workshops were organised and were well attended. There was a good level of participation in project excavations.

- A questionnaire survey of local attitudes to the heritage involving 120 postings achieved a 42% return. A majority of respondents thought that the landscape itself was the most important feature of the historic environment, (as opposed, for instance, to buildings or archaeological sites).

- An information panel was prepared as part of the project, to be sited close to Staunton-on-Arrow motte. This site had been the subject of vegetation clearance work.

Glossary

'Adaptive'
Term used in the Herefordshire Historic Landscape Characterisation for areas that consist of both *retentive* and *survey-planned* elements of landscape enclosure or contains more than one characteristic of *retentive* enclosure.

Alluvium
Term for sediment deposited by rivers, including that on the riverbed, along its margins and across its floodplain.

Anglo- Saxon
The period after the collapse of the Roman empire c. AD 410 to 1066. This period is often divided into early or migration period, middle Saxon and late Saxon. Also see *Dark Ages*.

Beaker
A late Neolithic and early Bronze Age ceramic vessel often highly decorated. The term is also used to define the general period in history during which this pottery is being produced between the late Neolithic and early Bronze Age (c. 2600- 1700BC).

Barrow
Upstanding remains usually of a burial mound. It is constructed by the up-cast of an external, usually circular, ditch being mounded up within the centre of the area defined by the ditch.

Black Burnished ware
A range of culinary and table wares that was manufactured during the Romano- British period between c.120AD and the late fourth century AD. Although a greyer form of this ware was made in the Thames Estuary area, much of the Black Burnished ware recovered came from the Dorest region.

Co-axial
Name given to a field system where the enclosure of the landscape is based on a regular field system which has a common plan and fairly tight structure. The framework of the enclosure consists of long, parallel but sinuous boundaries that form the axis to the system. These strips are then subdivided to create field plots. Such field systems began to be defined during the Bronze Age in Europe.

Colluvial deposits
Sediments washed down from hillslopes. These sediments effectively bury (seal and preserve) earlier deposits and land surfaces.

Cropmark
Variation in the growth of crops caused by disturbances in the soil due to features completely buried beneath. Cropmarks are most readily identified from the air under favourable lighting conditions.

Dark Ages
The period after the collapse of the Roman Empire c. AD 400 to the formation of the Anglo -Saxon kingdoms in the beginning of the 8th century.

Deposits
Archaeologically, significant traces that have been preserved, usually below ground, and from which it is possible to decipher sequences of past activities at or near the location in question.

Dirk
Extra long dagger, typically with a blade more than 200mm long.

Dyke
A linear earthwork comprising a bank or ditch, or both.

Early medieval
See *Anglo- Saxon.*

Earthwork
A general term describing any group of banks, ditches, mounds, scoops, hollows or platforms or other structures of earth and stone.

Enclosure
An area of land that is bounded by and defined by some kind of earthwork, fence, wall or defensive work. There is enormous variety in the shape, size, and scale of enclosures, as well as in their date and situation.

Established hedgerow
A hedgerow that contains mulitple hedging and tree species. The tree cover consists of substantial mature specimens.

Feature
Constituent part of an archaeological site or of the wider landscape.

Field Monument Warden
English Heritage staff charged with the monitoring of SAM condition and with the negotiation of Management Agreements with landowners.

Fill
Material deposited within an archaeological feature.

Funerary activity
Activity associated with the rites of death and burial of (or disposal of the remains of) members of a community.

Geomorphology
The study of the landscape and the processes that have shaped that the landscape whether this is due to natural or human interaction with the environment and the nature of the relationship between cultural and natural processes.

Geographic Information System
GIS. A map-based computerised archive and modelling system for geographical and related information.

Global Positioning System
GPS. Device used to provide geographic locations within the landscape through the use of satellite technology.

Ground Penetrating Radar
GPR. A method of geophysical survey that can be used to provide a three- dimensional view of a buried site. By traversing an area with a portable radar it is possible to produce, in visible form, vertical and horizontal profiles through buried deposits and remains.

Hillfort

An enclosure primarily of Iron Age (q.v) date, usually comprising at least one circuit of defensive bank and ditch. Usually sited on the crest of a hill, often with defences following a contour around the hilltop (hence, 'contour-defined hillfort').

Historic Environment

All the physical evidence for past human activity, and its associations, that people can see, feel, find and understand in the present world.

Historic Landscape Characterisation

HLC. An English Heritage sponsored project to understand the rural landscape and its pattern of enclosure in terms of its historical origins and its dominant characteristics.

Holloway

A track that, due to its location on a hill slope and in relatively soft geology, has through use become sunken into the ground, with high scarps on one or both sides.

Holocene

The later of two epochs forming the Quaternary Period, and dates from 10,000 years ago down to the present day.

House platform

A flat area created on sloping ground to form the foundation on which a structure could be built.

Inspector of Ancient Monuments

IAM. A member of staff of English Heritage with particular conservation responsibilites. At regional level, there are two Inspectors of Ancient Monuments for the West Midlands who routinely deal with SAM-based casework. These Inspectors work from the offices of the regional conservation team at Birmingham. One has responsibility for the counties of Herefordshire, Shropshire and Staffordshire.

Iron Age

The period c.800BC to the Roman conquest (locally c. AD 50-55).

Landscape Character Assessment

LCA. Mapping of the modern day landscape in terms of its geology and visible attributes such as topography, soil type, land use and hedgerows.

Leat

Artificial channel created to supply water from a natural source to a mill or other installation.

Medieval

Also Middle Ages. Defines the period between about AD 800 and roughly AD 1500.

Mesolithic

The period between the Palaeolithic and the Neolithic. This period is often associated with the end of the last Ice Age c. 12, 000 years ago to 4000 BC.

Midden

Essentially a dump of waste material, usually presumed to be domestic in character deriving from cooking or food processing activities. However recent research suggests that these deposits were often deliberately placed and 'symbolic'.

Mortaria

A stout mixing bowl, diagnostic of the Romano-British period. Interior surface contained coarse grit to assist in the preparation of foodstuffs and had a strong rim and pouring spout.

Mortuary area

Area, possibly with ritual significance, for the laying out of corpses before burial or any other form of disposal.

Motte and bailey

Medieval castle construction consisting of an earthern mound (motte) and a fortified enclosed courtyard surrounding the motte (bailey).

Neolithic

The period in England that sees the appearance of polished flint and stone axes, adzes and arrowheads and is generally associated with the introduction of cereal cultivation and animal domestication and the earliest production of pottery (c. 4000- 2000BC).

Palaeo-

Adjective prefix denoting that something is old or ancient; for instance, palaeochannel - an old river channel.

Palaeolithic

Period that spans nearly three and half million years from the evolution of the earliest humans to the end of the last glaciation. Generally divided into the Lower, Middle and Upper Palaeolithic.

Piedmont

Where a river system descends from an upland to a lowland topography.

Pillow mound

An artificial rabbit warren. This kind of earthwork feature usually comprises a ditched rectangular mound, and often containing covered runs and nesting boxes. Rabbits were farmed in such mounds in the period c.AD 1300-1700, both to contain the animals and protect them from predators.

Post medieval

Term describing the period after the medieval, generally after around AD 1540, until about AD 1750.

Quickset hedgerow

A hedgerow that consists mainly of a single species of hedging material, often set in geometric field pattern.

Resistivity survey

Geophysical survey used to locate buried features by mapping differences in the way that soils conduct an electric current.

'Retentive'

Term used in the Herefordshire Historic Landscape Characterisation to describe distinct areas of the landscape where an early established pattern of enclosure that has a definable genesis has been retained in an identifiable way (despite some redefinition of boundaries).

Radiocarbon dating

Also known as C^{14} dating. A technique of scientific dating that uses the natural decay of Carbon 14 isotopes within organic matter to determine its age.

Ring ditch
A bedrock or substrata cut ditch of circular plan, often only observed as a cropmark from the air. When excavated, ring ditches are usually found to be the ploughed-out remains of a *barrow*.

'Romanised'
Places, sites or structures that evince contact with and influence from the core areas of the Roman world. This influence is often registered by the adoption of Roman tastes or habits. It can include buildings with plastered walls, laid floors and tiled roofs, sometimes serviced by underfloor heating and bath suites.

Romano-British
The period locally from c.AD 50-55 until at least c.AD 410, during which time the county formed part of one of the provinces of the Roman Empire.

Samian ware
Roman mass produced pottery in a range of forms but characterised by glossy red glaze-like slip. Centres of production included northern Italy and southern part of Gaul.

Scheduled Ancient Monument
SAM. A monument designated in the national Schedule as a site of national importance.

Severn Valley ware
Burnished wares mainly bowls, jars and tankards often orange-red in colour made at various centres along the Severn dating to the Romano- British period. A centre of production is believed to exist near Malvern.

Section
Vertical side wall of an excavation trench, or vertical face cut through deposits or features, within an excavation trench to allow the study and recording of archaeological deposits.

Site
Any place where objects or features manufactured or modified by human beings are found.

'Survey- planned'
Term used in the Herefordshire Historic Landscape Characterisation for areas of landscape defined by the deliberate reconfiguration or new enclosure of the landscape for the purpose of agricultural improvement. This term is used because from c.AD 1700- 1850 at least, such laying out of the landscape was done from mapped surveys.

Trackway
Generally, an unsurfaced communications route linking one or more settlements, or settlements with related places such as fields or quarries.

Votive deposit
Deposition of an item, or even 'waste' material that has been made as an offering to gods spirits or ancestors

Ware
Ceramic products made of the same materials from a single production area, or vessels having the same basic characteristics or technique of manufacture.

Water Meadow
Area of grassland adjacent to a river or stream, artificially flooded and drained to promote enhanced grazing for livestock or the production of grass for hay.

APPENDIX 1

THE BEAKER POTTERY FROM THE GROVE, STAUNTON-ON-ARROW

Alex Gibson
Bradford University

Introduction

Four sherds plus six small fragments of pottery from Grove were sent to the writer for comment. These sherds were unpacked and laid out in good natural daylight for inspection. All sherds were examined macroscopically with the aid of a x10 handlense. No attempt at microscopic analysis has been made therefore the fabric descriptions are tentative and may be refined or redefined by microscopy.

The Grove

Fragments of four vessels have been identified. All are Beaker sherds: three are comb decorated and the fourth (vessel 1 in the catalogue) is incised. Vessel 3 is a flat-topped rim sherd. The vessels are described further in the catalogue.

Such small sherd material makes the reconstruction of the vessels difficult nevertheless, the narrow zoned decoration of vessels 2 and 4 may suggest stylistically early vessels. The zoned herring bone on vessel 4 might belong to Clarke's (1970) Basic European Motif Group 1 (motif 3) which he would see as commonly occurring on typologically early vessels. The broadness of the zone (over 17mm), the fineness of the fabric (only 3mm thick) and the well-defined combing might also suggest that this is indeed a typologically early vessel. It may perhaps even belong to Clarke's Wessex/Mid Rhine (W/MR) or North British/Mid Rhine (N/MR) or North Rhine (N/NR) groups. This would equate to step 3-4 of Lanting and van der Waals's scheme. It must be emphasised, however, that such an identification based on such a small sherds cannot be relied upon.

The zones of oblique lines on vessel 2 also belong to this early group (motif 2). The closeness of the zones on vessel 2, however, and the slightly raised areas between the zones may suggest that the sherd comes from a stylistically late vessel with contracted zones or with a complex decorative scheme (see Clarke 1970 fig.941). This vessel may perhaps even as late as Clarke's Late Southern (S3) style or Lanting and van der Waals' step 5 or 6.

The broad rim of vessel 3 and the deep zone of herring bone motif as well as the straight profile of the sherds also suggests a late vessel, perhaps similar, at least in upper outline, to the Late Northern (N3) vessel from Clinterty, Aberdeenshire (Clarke 1970, fig.661).

Discussion

Beakers from Herefordshire and the adjoining Welsh Marches are rare though this probably represents a lack of antiquarian interest rather than a true distribution. The present vessels, therefore, make a valuable addition to the existing frugal corpus. The vessels from Olchon, Hereford, like vessel 1 from Little Garway, are simply decorated and belong to Clarke's N/MR group which may possibly support the identifications offered here. The material from Merlin's Cave, Ross on Wye is too fragmentary for reconstruction while that from Mathon (Clarke 1970 No.356), a Late Southern style (S3) vessel is decorated with a complex combination of repeated filled triangles. The dagger burial at Aymestrey was associated with comb-zoned Beaker of Clarke's Primary North-British/Dutch group (Woodiwiss 1989).

The rich Beaker burial from Wellington Quarry, Marden (Harrison *et al.* 1999) contained a stylistically very early Beaker identified by Harrison as belonging to the All Over Ornamented Group or Clarke's European Group (ibid 5). It is however a zone decorated Beaker with zones of oblique comb impressions separated by spaced horizontal lines and undecorated bands. The everted and thinned rim of the Wellington vessel and its simple, narrow zone decoration matches that from Garway.

The dating of this material is difficult given the small sherd material and the lack of reconstructable profiles and decorative schemes. Furthermore, the systematic dating of Beaker burials has shown that Beakers of various styles were in contemporaneous use (Kinnes *et al.* 1991) irrespective of whether the Clarke scheme, the steps of Lanting and van der Waals or the stages of Case (1977) are used. Dates for the stylistically later styles, probably represented by the Grove material appear to span the period 2500-1700 Cal BC.

Using radiocarbon dating and associated artefacts, Needham (1996) has suggested that early (formative) Beakers belong to his Bronze Age period 1 (2500-2300 Cal BC) while developed Beakers (floruit) belong to period 3 (2300-2050 Cal BC) and the late (late) style vessels belong to his period 3 (2010-1700 Cal BC). The majority of Beaker radiocarbon dates span the period 2300-1700 Cal BC. The Grove material may belong to the later period, sometime after 2000 Cal BC.

CATALOGUE

GROVE 2003

CONTEXT
VESSEL NO DESCRIPTION

202
1   Single sherd in a smooth, soft, grog-filled fabric with reddish-brown surfaces and a black core. There appear to be faint herring bone incisions or impressions on the outer surface.

205
2   One large sherd and five crumbs of Beaker. The fabric is smooth, well-fired and contains grog inclusions. The outer surface is well-finished and reddish brown while the inner surface is dark grey-brown and the core is black. The decoration on the outer surface comprises the remains of three spaced rows of fine toothed comb ladder motif.

205
3   Two sherds in a soft, smooth and well-fired fabric containing grog inclusions. The outer surface is well-finished and reddish brown while the inner surface is dark grey-brown and the core is black. The decoration, on the outer surface, comprises 1.5 lines of herringbone motif in close-set toothed comb. The comb has been short with square sectioned teeth. The larger sherd preserves a flat-topped rim.

206
4   Single fine, well-fired sherd with a smooth, reddish-brown outer surface, grey-brown inner surface and black core. The fabric contains grog. Decoration on the outer surface comprises a zone of herring bone motif of toothed comb impressions. It would appear that the comb used for the encircling line below the zone has had more square-sectioned teeth than that used to form the herring bone.

APPENDIX 2

A Middle Bronze Age Dirk/Dagger from Windmill Hill, Eardisland, Herefordshire

Martyn Barber
English Heritage, Swindon

Principal Measurements of dirk/ dagger

Maximum (original) length = 195mm
Maximum butt width = 33mm
Thickness (butt) = 3.5mm
Thickness (blade mid-point) = 3mm
Thickness (blade tip) = 1.5mm
Weight = 51g

Description

The object is near complete, some minor loss occurring along both blade edges and close to one of the shoulder points of the butt. When viewed, the object had not been fully cleaned of soil, but it seems unlikely that any significant detail has been obscured. Overall, the metal is a brown-bronze colour with the odd greener patch showing, the latter most notable on the faces of the butt and along the blade edges in places.

The butt itself is rounded or arched at the end, though straightening on both sides towards the point where the blade begins. The butt surface is flat on both faces, and featureless with the exception of a few minor dents on one face.

No rivet holes are present in the butt. A semi-circular notch, presumably representing the intended location of a rivet in order to hold the blade within a hilt, is present along one edge, roughly at the point where the arched or rounded end of the butt would have met the straighter side. A slighter and less regular indentation just below this *may* represent a remnant of another notch, but seems more likely to be post-depositional damage. When present, rivets tend to be of copper alloy also, but none were reported by the finder. There is no trace of a hilt mark. Any hilt is likely to have been made from organic material such as wood or bone. If one was present at the point of deposition, its survival would clearly be dependent on the nature of the burial environment

The blade is fairly narrow, its width decreasing markedly just below the butt before tapering more gently towards the blade tip. The blade appears to broaden slightly below its mid-point before narrowing again towards the tip. While this may be partly a result of post-depositional loss of blade edges, it does appear to be a genuine if slight original feature. More distinctly leaf-shaped blades are not unknown among objects of this type. The blade features on both faces a broad and very slightly rounded central section, the two appearing to be very slightly offset from one another in places. On both faces, the central section stands circa 1mm above the adjacent edge bevel.

The blade itself is no longer flat, having been bent at 3 points along its length and, probably as a consequence, slightly twisted. The first bend occurs circa 55mm from the arched tip of the butt, and is the most prominent. The other two, far less noticeable, occur circa 45mm from the first and circa 50mm from the blade tip respectively. It is possible that only the first was intentional, the lower bends (and the slight twisting) occurring as a result of the manner in which the blade was held during the process of attempting to bend it. This bending and twisting almost certainly occurred prior to deposition. There are no visible signs of damage or stress to the blade at any of the bends. When laid flat, the blade rests on its central portion, the butt and blade tip being raised.

The blade edges and tip seem reasonably intact, post-depositional loss apart, although there are one or two slight notches that may have occurred prior to deposition. No traces of the casting process are visible – the full range of post-casting activities appear to have been completed, leaving a fully finished object (though see comments about the hilt arrangement below). It seems likely that the edges had been sharpened and were largely intact when deposited.

Discussion

According to established typological practice, the object should be classified as a dirk, and assigned to Burgess and Gerloff's (1981) Group IV. More than half of all British and Irish finds of dirks and rapiers fall within this Group, which simply comprises all blades with a flattened or slightly rounded centre section. Burgess and Gerloff's scheme, based on an earlier classification scheme proposed by Burgess (1968), focuses on blade forms and cross-sections, features that Burgess and Gerloff (1981, 3) argued "are normally immutable". Far greater variety is evident among butt forms, numbers and arrangements of rivet holes or notches, and blade length.

Four broad groups were identified by Burgess and Gerloff (1981), Group IV being both the largest (in terms of the number of objects assigned to it) and, typologically speaking, the latest. The Eardisland blade belongs to Group IV by virtue of its flattish centre section. The butt form of the Eardisland example is harder to match precisely among the numerous Group IV weapons, although if one ignores notches and rivet holes, the arrangement of arched terminal and straight sides is far from uncommon.

It is not unusual to encounter difficulties in identifying precise parallels among the extant corpus for new finds of dirks or rapiers – as Burgess and Gerloff (1981, 5) noted, "practically none of the thousand or so dirks and rapiers can be shown to have been cast in the same mould". This is not the same as saying that none were ever cast in the same mould, but the probable use in most instances of clay moulds, which could be used only once, underlines the fact that most bladed weapons of Middle and Late Bronze Age date were individual castings, something that would help to account for the seemingly endless minor variations around a small number of common features.

A brief word about nomenclature may be necessary at this point. Typologically speaking, the object should be classed as a dirk, although this term need have no bearing on precise function. The history of attempts to classify dirks and rapiers is summarised by Burgess and Gerloff (1981, 1-5). Here it will suffice to point out that both terms – 'dirk' and 'rapier' – appear to have been intended as merely descriptive terms, the latter applied to long, narrow blades better suited to a thrusting motion; the latter to shorter, narrow bladed weapons which could be distinguished from the main series of daggers of the Early to Middle Bronze Age. The line drawn between dirks and rapiers is purely arbitrary, and was established initially by Trump (1962, 84), who defined a rapier as any narrow-bladed weapon longer than 35.5cm, while dirks comprised those

between 21.6cm and 35.5cm. Anything below 21.6cm was classed as a dagger seemingly irrespective of form. Trump argued that these were meaningful divisions, although it was based on a sample of just 100 weapons. Burgess and Gerloff (1981) examined nearly 1000 blades and noted "no marked dividing line" (ibid, 5), instead selecting their own "purely arbitrary figure of 30cm to divide dirks from rapiers on the basis that those shorter than this can generally have been used for stabbing and as versatile weapons and implements which could have fulfilled the many functions of daggers and knives. Those above 30cm are generally seen to be less versatile in size and proportions, and to be more specifically intended as thrusting weapons" (ibid.). Burgess and Gerloff ignored the lower limit set by Trump for dirks, and in their corpus around 20% of the weapons assigned to their Group IV are less than 21.6cm in length. Moreover, in an assessment of total lengths of all Group IV implements in their corpus for which an accurate assessment of original total length can be made, more than half measure between 25 and 40 centimetres, and around a third are between 10 and 25 centimetres, with no clear break in the distribution. If anything, the length measurement peaks at around 30cm, the point at which Burgess and Gerloff established their dividing line. The Eardisland implement therefore would, on the basis of Trump's measurements, best be described as a dagger. In Burgess and Gerloff's scheme, it is a dirk, lying within the bottom 20% in terms of total length.

Pushing typological niceties to one side, as a fairly short, lightweight, double edged blade, the Eardisland 'dirk' is likely to have functioned best as a hand-held knife or dagger, the length and shape of the blade best suited to a stabbing or thrusting motion when used in anger. Assessments of function based on form are not without their problems, of course (see Barber 2003, Ch. 5). Some of the small nicks along the blade of the Eardisland example may well be pre-depositional, and if they were not inflicted at the same time that the blade was being bent, then they may well indicate use in a slashing or cutting motion (which, of course, need not have occurred in the course of a violent act).

There remain important question marks over the precise function of the Eardisland dirk, however. As is noted above, the butt and upper blade bear no trace of a hilt. Moreover, the single notch raises questions about how any hilt might have been attached to the dirk. If we assume that no metal rivets were missed by the original finder, then there is a strong possibility that the dirk was deposited in an unhafted state. This would by no means be an unusual state of affairs – many of the bronzes deposited at Flag Fen near Peterborough (Pryor 2001), for example, must have been deposited without hafts, as the conditions at that site mean that any attached organic haft would have survived. Furthermore, some dirks and rapiers were actually worked after casting in such a way that a hilt could never have been attached (see e.g. Needham 1990).

Mention of Flag Fen, of course, raises the issue of how the Eardisland dirk came to be deposited in the first place. The idea of votive deposition, particularly in or close to wet contexts (lakes, rivers, streams, springs, bogs etc), is one with a long if chequered history in British archaeology (Bradley 1990; Barber 2003 Ch. 2), but has been increasingly accepted in recent years although the precise motives for such deposition remain a matter for debate. For dirks and rapiers, Burgess and Gerloff (1981, 5) estimated that more than 85% of the 1000 or so British and Irish examples that they catalogued had been found in wet contexts. Subsequent discoveries have done little to alter this situation. The possibility that the Eardisland dirk was purposely deposited unhafted, in a damp environment, after being deliberately bent (i.e. rendered unusable) seems perfectly plausible on the basis of the available evidence, and fits in well with what is known more generally about the dirks and rapiers of the Middle Bronze Age.

Dating such objects is difficult. As would be expected of objects generally found in wet places, most have occurred as single finds. Associations with other independently datable material are highly unusual though by no means unknown (Burgess and Gerloff 1981, 105ff). The few definite hoard associations from across the British Isles as a whole would support suggestions that most Group IV weapons belong somewhere in the Taunton or Penard stages of Bronze Age metalworking. The current dating of those phases, based on radiocarbon dating rather than typology (Needham et al 1997), spans the period c1400 to c1140 BC, a range which spans much of the Middle Bronze Age. Greater precision would only be possible had some organic material suitable for radiocarbon dating been found both in situ and in direct association with the dirk.

Had such a means of dating been available, then one niggling doubt about the date of deposition might have been removed. It is becoming increasingly clear that during the Bronze Age a small but significant proportion of objects were not finally deposited until some considerable time after they were made. A key example here is the Group IV dirk/rapier, slightly longer than the Eardisland example, found at Danebury hillfort, Hampshire (Cunliffe 1984, 335-340) along with other bronzes presumed to represent a hoard that cannot have been buried until after 800 BC.

In the British Isles, finds of Group IV dirks and rapiers are quite widespread, but with notable concentrations in the Thames Valley and the Fens of East Anglia. In the broader region around Eardisland, such items are rather thin on (or in) the ground. The nearest find of a Group IV weapon seems likely to be the fragmentary item from the hoard found at Ffynhonnau, Brecon (Burgess and Gerloff 1981 no. 804), while a few fragments of Group IV weapons have been reported recently from Swansea Bay (www.finds.org.uk and Adam Gwilt pers. comm.). Crossing the Severn, the nearest examples known come from Bath and from Bromham, Wiltshire (Burgess and Gerloff 1981 nos. 570A and 661). As a Group IV dirk, then, the Eardisland example is currently rather isolated.

APPENDIX 3

The Iron Age and Romano-British pottery from sites in the Arrow Valley, Herefordshire

C. Jane Evans

Summary

All four Arrow Valley sites produced pottery. The Leen (LEE 03) assemblage dated mainly to the late Iron Age, although a few sherds of poorly dated Roman pottery were recorded. The other sites produced Romano-British pottery. The largest group (119 sherds), from The Leen Middle Fields (LMF 03), dated to between the second and fourth centuries. The Leen Top Hayles (LTH 03) and The Grove (GRO 03) produced much smaller assemblages, with poor dating evidence.

Methodology

The pottery was recorded with reference to the Worcestershire County Fabric Series (Table 1), formerly the Herefordshire and Worcestershire County Series, prefixed WCMF in the tables (Hurst and Rees 1992, 200-209). Where possible the National Roman Fabric Reference Collection (Tomber and Dore 1998), the Kenchester fabric series (Tomber 1985, fiche frames 1-12), and the *Ariconium* fabric series (Willis forthcoming) were also cross referenced. Fabrics that correlate directly with the National Series are highlighted in bold in table 1 below. Those that did not were allocated a site specific code derived from the national system. The assemblage is quantified by sherd count, weight and rim EVE (estimated vessel equivalent, Tables 2 and 3). Base EVEs are recorded in the archive. Precise form types and broad vessel classes (for example bowl, cook pot) were recorded, together with any evidence for decoration, manufacture, repair, use or reuse. Much of the pottery was very abraded. The data was recorded on an Access database.

Fabrics

The fabrics reaching the site indicated a variety of sources. The Iron Age pottery came from the Malvern Hills (Peacock 1968), to the east, and the

Table 1: List of fabrics represented

Common Name	WCMF Fabric Code	National Code (Bold)/Local code	Kenchester Code	Ariconium Code	Description/references (T&D = Tomber and Dore 1998)
Malvernian group A, handmade	3	**MAL RE A**	Malv. HM	G11	T&D 147, plate 120; Peacock 1967, Peacock 1968
Mudstone tempered ware	9	NAT MD	Mudstone	-	Hurst and Rees 1992, 202; Morris Group D 1982, 15-6; Morris 1983; Morris 1992; Tomber 1985, 103
Severn Valley ware	12	**SVW OX 2**	SVW	O10-O24	Standard oxidised fabric, unsourced: T&D 149, Pl 122; Webster 1976, Rawes 1982
Severn Valley ware, reduced	12.1	SVW RE	Grey ware	R20, R24,R33	Standard fabric, reduced
Organic tempered SVW	12.2	SVW ORG OX			Organic tempered variant, oxidised (elongated voids appearing as black/dark grey streaks in fracture).
Fine, organic tempered SVW	12.21	SVW ORG OX		?O18, ?O22	Fine organic tempered, cf Evans et al. 2000, 17 fabrics O1 and O5?
South-east Dorset BB1	22	**DOR BB 1**	BB1	B11	T&D 127, pl 100; Williams 1977; Seager Smith and Davies, 1993
Mancetter Hartshill mortarium	32	**MAH WH**	Man		T&D 189, pl 157a-d; Tomber 1985 fiche, 12
Oxfordshire white mortarium	38	**OXF WH**	Oxford WW	M25	T&D 174, pls 145-6 a-b; Tomber 1985 fiche, 11
Severn Valley mortarium	110	**CAR CC**	Caerleon	M40	T&D 204, pl 170, Tomber 1985 fiche 12
Samian	43	SA	-	-	
Central Gaulish Samian	43.21	**LMV SA**	CG samian	S02	T&D , 30. pl 19

Table 2: Summary of the pottery assemblages by fabric

WCMF

Code	LEE			LMF			LTH			GRO		
	Qty	WT.	RE	Qty	Wt.	RE	Qty	Wt.	R.E	Qty	Wt.	RE
12	28	175	2	44	594	37	13	51	0	19	33	0
12.1	-	-	-	6	53	15	-	-	-	-	-	-
12.2	-	-	-	2	12	0	5	22	0	-	-	-
12.21	-	-	-	5	67	0	3	24	0	-	-	-
3	3	34	0	1	19	0	-	-	-	-	-	-
9	64	133	10	-	-	-	-	-	-	-	-	-
22	2	5	0	45	429	43	-	-	-	-	-	-
32	-	-	-	1	9	0	-	-	-	-	-	-
38	-	-	-	-	-	-	-	-	-	1	12	5
110	-	-	-	1	32	9	-	-	-	-	-	-
43	-	-	-	3	7	0	1	12	0	-	-	-
43.21	-	-	-	11	64	0	-	-	-	1	1	0

Martley area (Morris 1982, 1983), to the north east. The Romano-British assemblage was dominated by regionally produced wares, in particular Severn Valley ware in a variety of variants. The precise source or sources of this ware are uncertain. A number of kilns are known at Malvern and Leigh Sinton, to the east of the Malverns (Evans et al. 2000, 70-1). In Herefordshire, a late Roman kiln has been excavated at Stoke Prior (Haliwell 1991; SMR 33843), and other kilns are suspected at Marley Hall near Ledbury (SMR 6800 4000), and Cradley (SMR 5462). There may well be undiscovered Severn Valley ware production sites in Herefordshire, though further research is required to assess this. A range of the more widely traded Roman wares was also present. Sources included Dorset (BB1), Mancetter Hartshill in the West Midlands, and Oxfordshire. Small quantities of imported samian, including some Les Martres-de-Veyre in Central Gaul, were also represented.

The Leen, Middle Fields (LMF 03)

Excavation at The Leen, Middle Fields produced the largest of the four assemblages (Table 2). Romano-British pottery was recovered from the upper part of a number of fills (102, 111, 114, and 115) in the north-south ditch in Trench 1. The small assemblage (29 sherds) included some diagnostically second to third century Severn Valley ware forms: a bowl (Evans et al. 2000, fig. 29 type 4) and a jar (Webster 1976, types A5, A6, A8). These provide a rather broad TPQ for the assemblage. The presence of BB1 (102, 114) normally suggests a date around c AD 120 or later, although it was very poorly represented (1% by weight) and small quantities can reach this area earlier than this. The overall range of fabrics (Figure 1) suggests an emphasis on second century, and perhaps earlier, material (Figure 1). The assemblage was dominated by Severn Valley ware (Figure 1; WCMF 12, 12.1, 12.2 and 12.21), including the organic tempered variant (WCMF 12.2). The latter generally dates to the first to second century, although the finer variant (WCMF 12.21) has been associated with second and third century vessels elsewhere (Evans et al. 2000, 17). A body sherd in Malvernian ware (111) is probably from a tubby cooking pot, also dating to the first or second century (Peacock 1967, 15-18). Three sherds of samian were present. These were all much abraded and were not precisely identified. They date to some time in the first or second century. The shallow deposit along the eastern side of the ditch (122) produced a base from a BB1 bowl or dish, only broadly datable to the second to fourth century.

The pit at the northern side of the trench produced a sequence of fills containing Roman pottery (44 sherds). The primary fill (116) contained two sherds of BB1, a sherd of Severn Valley ware (WCMF 12) and two sherds of reduced Severn Valley ware (WCMF 12.1). The latter included the bead rim from a wide mouthed jar, dating to the mid to late second century (Webster 1976, fig. 4, type C21). The three layers above this (117, 118, 119) provided little dating evidence. The only identifiable forms were two plain rimmed, BB1 dishes, of a type

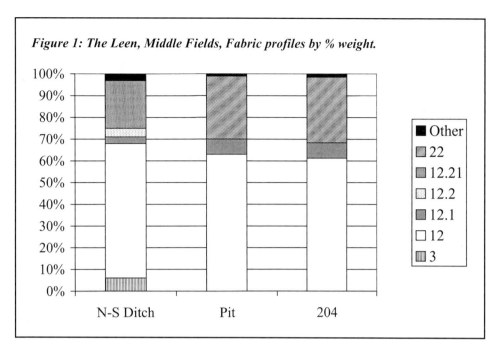

Figure 1: The Leen, Middle Fields, Fabric profiles by % weight.

produced throughout the Roman period (Seager Smith and Davies 1993, type 20). The only other pottery comprised undiagnostic body sherds in Severn Valley ware. The largest group (26 sherds) came from the uppermost fill (120), including some quite substantial fragments. A TPQ for this deposit was provided by a BB1 flange rimmed bowl, dating to some time after c AD 270 (Seager Smith and Davies 1993, fig. 124 type 25; Holbrook and Bidwell 1991, 99). Another BB1 form, a bead rimmed dish, dated to some time after the mid second century (Holbrook and Bidwell 1991, fig. 32 57.4). Less diagnostic sherds included Severn Valley ware (WCMF 12, 12.1) and a sherd from a Mancetter Hartshill mortarium (WCMF 32). The pit did not contain any of the characteristically early fabrics present in the north-south ditch (WCMF 3, 12.2), and the later emphasis is reflected in the relatively higher proportion of BB1 (Figure 1).

The latest feature in Trench 1 was a shallow east-west ditch. This produced only three fragmentary

and abraded sherds of Roman pottery. This supports the interpretation of this as a more modern feature.

Excavation in Trench 2 revealed two parallel ditches, both of which produced Roman pottery. The largest group (30 sherds) came from fill 204. This included a number of datable forms. A flat rimmed bowl (Seager Smith and Davies 1993, fig. 123, type 22; Holbrook and Bidwell 1991, 109, figs. 30 and 31) indicated a TPQ some time from the mid second to mid third century. An upright rimmed jar dated to the second century (Seager Smith and Davies 1993, fig. 122, type 1), and a Severn Valley ware tankard (Webster 1976, fig. 7, type E39, E40) to the second to third century. The relative proportion of BB1 and Severn Valley ware was similar to the Trench 1 pit assemblage (Figure 1). The other fill (202) produced fragments from a samian Drag 18/31 bowl, probably from Les Martres-de-Veyre in Central Gaul, dating to c AD 100-120 (Webster 1996, 35). The only other sherd was the rim of a

Table 3: The Leen, Middle Fields, summary of the Romano-British pottery by feature

Trench EVE	Feature Description	Qty	% Qty	Wt. (g)	% Wt.	Av. Sherd Wt. (g)	RimEve	% Rim
1	N-S ditch	29	24	307	24	11	29	28
1	Pit	44	37	601	47	14	37	35.5
1	E-W Ditch	3	3	7	<1	2	0	0
1	Shallow feature	1	<1	5	<1	5	0	0
2	Ditch	42	35	366	28	9	38	36.5

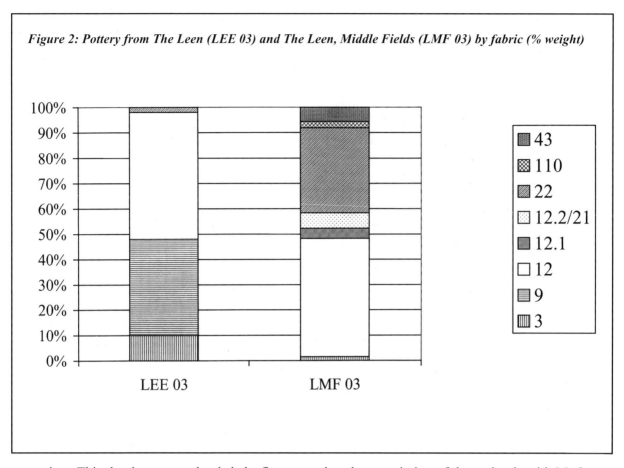

Figure 2: Pottery from The Leen (LEE 03) and The Leen, Middle Fields (LMF 03) by fabric (% weight)

Legend:
- 43
- 110
- 22
- 12.2/21
- 12.1
- 12
- 9
- 3

mortarium. This sherd was very abraded, the flange was incomplete, and few trituration grits survived, all hindering precise identification. It is probably a Caerleon product (WCMF 110). The upstanding rim, and what survives of the flange, is similar to an example published from 22 High Street, Leintwardine (Hartley 1996, fig 12.19), dated c AD 115-160. A Caerleon mortarium is recorded from Kenchester, dated by Kay Hartley to c AD 140-170 (Tomber 1985, fiche fig. 17 133.1). It is also recorded from Ariconium (Willis forthcoming) where it is broadly dated to c AD 75-190, though no forms are illustrated.

The Leen (LEE 03)

The fabric profile for this site is quite distinct from The Leen, Middle Fields, with an emphasis on native, Iron Age fabrics (Figure 2). The upper fill of the Trench 1 ditch (102) produced body sherds of mudstone tempered ware (WCMF 9; Morris 1982, group D; Tomber 1985, 103), with a probable source in the Martley area, and base sherds in Malvernian fabric A (WCMF 3). The latter was produced into the Roman period (Peacock 1967),

but the association of these sherds with Mudstone tempered ware suggests that they too are Iron Age in date (Peacock 1968, 415-421; Tomber 1985, 102-3). Both of these fabrics are noted at Croft Ambrey (Stanford 1974, 191-2, Malvernian and 'vesicular'), Lyonshall (Richardson 1983, fabrics IA and MVW) and Kenchester, as well as a number of other sites in the Welsh Marches (Tomber 1985, 111-3). However, Ariconium, to the south, seems to be outside the distribution area (Willis forthcoming). The Iron Age sherds all came from the lower part of fill 102, and were all very fragmentary (average sherd weight 3g). The upper part of the fill produced ten, fragmentary and abraded sherds of Severn Valley ware (WCMF 12). The only form sherd was a simple, out-turned rim from a jar or bowl, possibly dating to the first or second century (cf Webster 1976, fig. 4 C19, C20).

Only the upper two fills of the Trench 2 ditch produced pottery (202, 203), including further fragmentary sherds of mudstone-tempered ware. The lower fill (203) produced only this ware (average sherd weight 4g), including an everted rim from a jar. This is a typically Late Iron Age form; similar vessels are noted in Palaeozoic limestone ware from late Iron Age and conquest period contexts at Beckford, Worcestershire (Ford and Rees 1984, form 10; Evans 1990, 31 phases E and F). Nearby in Herefordshire, a similar form is recorded from Lyonshall (Richardson 2003, fig. 3.1, 2). The upper of these fills (202) produced further sherds of Iron Age, mudstone tempered ware (average sherd weight 1g), associated with substantial amounts of charcoal. This fill also produced a small quantity of Roman pottery; Severn Valley ware (WCMF 12, 18 sherds) and BB1 (WCMF 22, 2 sherds). There were no datable forms. The presence of BB1 might indicate a TPQ of c AD 120, though small quantities were reaching sites in this region before this.

The Leen, Top Hales (LTH 03)

Excavation at The Leen produced a small assemblage of 22 sherds, all from silt deposits sealing the barrow ditch. These were all very fragmentary and abraded. Three layers (208, 209, and 232) produced sherds of Severn Valley ware, only broadly datable to the Roman period. Another (226) produced an equally abraded sherd of samian from a decorated form. The precise fabric of this has not been identified, and it is only broadly dated to the first or second century. Another deposit (222) produced four sherds of Severn Valley ware, three in the characteristically early organic variant (WCMF 12.2). While this small assemblage is indicative of some level of Roman activity in the vicinity, it does not indicate any significant Roman activity on the site itself.

The Grove (GRO 03)

Excavation at The Grove also produced a very small assemblage. Five sherds from Trench 1 came from a layer overlying the primary ditch fill (102, 107). All were very fragmentary and abraded, with no diagnostic forms. Four sherds of Severn Valley ware were only broadly dateable to the Roman period. A sherd of samian was possibly from Les Martres-de-Veyre, indicating a date between c AD 100-120. In Trench 2, fragments of abraded Severn Valley ware were recovered from two contexts (201, 202). These were again only dateable to the Roman period. In Trench 3, the upper fill of the inner enclosure ditch (302) produced a single sherd of Oxfordshire white mortaria. The flange on this was missing, precluding precise identification. The ware was produced from c AD 100 and throughout the Roman period.

Bibliography

Bannister, A.T. 1916. *The Place-Names of Herefordshire. Their Origins and Development.* Cambridge University Press. Cambridge

Bapty, I. 2000. Understanding the Dynamics of Physical Change on Historic Earthworks: Analysing Patterns of Long-Term Erosion on Offa's Dyke, in: McGlade, D. (ed.) *Erosion Control on Archaeological Earthworks and Recreational Paths.* Northumberland County Council. Northumberland, 51- 57

Barber, M. 2003. Bronze and the Bronze Age: metalwork and society in Britain c2500-800 BC. Tempus Publishing Ltd, Stroud.

Berry, A. 2000. Resourcing of Managament Objectives: The Opportunities of Agri-environment Schemes, in: McGlade, D. (ed.) *Erosion Control on Archaeological Earthworks and Recreational Paths.* Northumberland County Council. Northumberland, 63- 68

Bevan, V.O., Davies, J. and Haverfield, F. 1896. *An Archaeological Survey of Herefordshire.* Society of Antiquaries. London

Brown, A. G. and Keough, M. K. 1992. Palaeochannels and palaeosurfaces: the geoarchaeological potential of some Midland floodplains, in: Needham, S. and Macklin, M. G. (eds.) *Alluvial Archaeology in Britain.* Oxbow Press. Oxford, 85- 196

Bradley, R. 1990. The Passage of Arms. An rchaeological analysis of hoards and votive deposits. Cambridge University Press, Cambridge

Burgess, C. 1968. Bronze Age Dirks and Rapiers as illustrated by examples from Durham and Northumberland. Transactions of the Architectural and Archaeological Society of Durham and Northumberland, New Series vol **1**, 3-26

Burgess, C and S Gerloff. 1981. The Dirks and Rapiers of Great Britain and Ireland. Prähistorische Bronzefunde IV,7; C.H. Beck, Munich

Case, H. 1977. The Beaker Cultures in Britain and Ireland, in Mrecer, R. J. (ed), *Beakers in Britain and Europe*, 71-101. BAR International Series No.**26**, Oxford: British Archaeological Reports

Clarke, D.L. 1970. *Beaker Pottery of Great Britain and Ireland.* Cambridge: Cambridge University Press

Coplestone- Crow, B. 1989. *Herefordshire Place-Names.* BAR British Series **214**. Oxford

Cunliffe, B. 1984. Danebury: An Iron Age Hillfort in Hampshire. Volume 2. The Excavations 1969-1978: The Finds. CBA Research Report **52**; CBA, York

Dalwood, H. and Atkins. M. 1998. *The Impact of Extensive Urban Survey in Hereford and Worcester.* Hereford and Worcester County Archaeological Service, Report **608**

Darvill, T. 1992. *Prehistoric Britain.* Batsford. London

Darvill, T. 2002. *Oxford Concise Dictionary of Archaeology.* Oxford University Press. Oxford

Dinn, J. 1995a. *Marches Uplands Survey:Nash transect.* Hereford and Worcester County Council, Report **132**

Dinn, J. 1995b. *Marches Uplands Survey: Herrock Hill transect.* Hereford and Worcester County Council, Report **133**

Dinn, J. 1995c. *Marches Uplands Survey:Hergest Ridge transect.* Hereford and Worcester County Council, Report **134**

Dinn, J. 1996. *Alluvial archaeology in the Herefordshire valleys: an assessment of survey techniques and archaeological potential.* Hereford and Worcester County Council, Report **456**

Dinn, J. and Edwards, R. 1999. *The Marches Upland Survey.* County Archaeological Service, Worcestershire County Council Report **500**. Worcester

Dinn, J. and Roseff, R. 1992. Alluvium and Archaeology in the Herefordshire Valleys, in: Needham, S. and Macklin, M. G. (eds.) *Alluvial Archaeology in Britain.* Oxbow Press. Oxford, 141-151

Dwerryhouse, A. R. and Miller, A. A. 1930. Glaciation of Clun Forest, Radnor Forest and some adjoining areas. *Quarterly Journal of the Geological Society of London*, **86**, 96-129.

Edwards, P. 1991. *Farming: Sources for Local Historians.* Batsford. London

English Heritage. 1999. *Scheduled Monuments. A guide for owners and occupiers.* English Heritage. London

English Heritage. 2000. *Power of Place.* English Heritage. London

Evans, C. J. 1990, The pottery, in J Dinn and J Evans 1990, Aston Mill Farm, Kemerton: Excavation of a Ring-ditch, Middle Iron Age Enclosures, and a *Grubenhaus, Trans. Worcestershire Archaeol. Soc. 3rd Ser.* **12**, 26-39

Evans, C. J., Jones, L. and Ellis, P. 2000, *Severn Valley Ware Production at Newland Hopfields. Excavation of a Romano-British kiln site at North End Farm, Great Malvern, Worcestershire in 1992 and 1994*, BAR British Ser. 313, Birmingham University Field Archaeology Unit Monogr. Ser. **2**

Farquhar-Oliver, P. 2003, *The Parliamentary Enclosures of Herefordshire.* Unpublished manuscript, copy in Herefordshire SMR

Fleming, A. 1988. *The Dartmoor Reeves. Investigating Prehistoric Land Divisions.* Batsford. London

Feryok, M. 2001. Offa's Dyke, in: Zaluckyj, S. *Mercia: The Anglo-Saxon Kingdom of Central England.* Logaston Press. Herefordshire, 163- 192

Ford, D and Rees, H 1984, The Iron Age and later pottery from Beckford, unpublished typescript, Worcestershire County Council

Fox. C. 1955. *Offa's Dyke: A Field Survey of the Western Frontier- Works of Mercia in the Seventh and Eighth Centuries.* Oxford University Press. Oxford

French, C., Macklin, M. G. and Passmore, D. G. 1992. Archaeology and palaeochannels in the Lower Welland and Nene valleys: alluvial archaeology at the Fen-edge, eastern England, in: Needham, S. and Macklin, M. G. (eds.) *Alluvial Archaeology in Britain.* Oxbow Press. Oxford, 169-176

Gelling, M. and Cole, A. 2000. *The Landscape of Place-Names.* Shaun Tyas. Stamford

Gibson, A. 1999. *TheWalton Basin Project: Excavation and Survey in a Prehistoric Landscape, 1993- 7.* Council for British Archaeology. Research Report **118**. York

Grey, Howard Levi. 1915. *English Field Systems.* Harvard University Press (London: Merlin Press reprint, 1959)

Guest, P. *forthcoming.* Lost Horizons: Archaeology of the Iron Age/ Roman Transition. In: White, R. (ed) *A Clash of Cultures? - Research into the Romano-British period in the West Midlands. The Making of the West Midlands* **3**

Haliwell, P. R. (ed.) 1991, Herefordshire Archaeological News **55**, 31.

Hartley, K. F. 1996, Mortaria, in D. L. Brown, The Roman small town at Leintwardine: excavations and other fieldwork 1971-1989, *Transactions of the Woolhope Naturalists' Field Club*, **48**, 510-572

Harrison, R.J., Jackson, R. and Napthan, M. 1999. A Rich Bell Beaker burial from Wellington Quarry, Marden, Herefordshire. *Oxford Journal of Archaeology*, **18. 1**, 1-16

Hill, D. and Worthington, M. 2003. *Offa's Dyke. History and Guide.* Tempus. Stroud

Holbrook, N. and Bidwell, P. T. 1991, *Roman finds from Exeter*, Exeter Archaeol. Rep., **4**, Exeter.

Hurst, D. and Rees, H. 1992, Pottery fabrics; a multi-period series for the County of Hereford and Worcester, in S. Woodiwiss (ed.) 1992, *Iron Age and Roman salt production and the medieval town of Droitwich*, CBA Res. Rep. **81**, 200-209

Jackson, R. *forthcoming*. Pits, Pots, Places and People: approaching the Neolithic at Wellington Quarry, in Garwood. P. (ed) *The Undiscovered Country. The earlier prehistory of the West Midlands. The Making of the West Midlands* **1**

Jago, M. 1995. The Countryside Stewardship Scheme: Testing the Way Forward for Integrated Countryside Management, in: Berry, A. and Brown, I. W. (eds) *Managing Ancient Monuments: An Integrated Approach.* Clwyd County Council. Clwyd, 49- 60

Kinnes, I.A., Gibson, A.M., Ambers, J., Bowman, S., Leese, M. & Boast, R. 1991. Radiocarbon Dating and British Beakers: The British Museum Programme. *Scottish Archaeological Review*, **8**, 35-68

Lanting, J.N. & van der Waals, J.D. 1972. British Beakers as seen from the Continent. *Helinium*, 12, 20-46

Lello, R. 2003. *Mowley Wood, Staunton-on-Arrow: Woodland Survey.* Herefordshire Archaeology Report **88**. Hereford

Lias, A. 1991. *Place Names of the Welsh Borderlands*. Orphans Press. Leominster

Lewis, B. n.d. *Boundary Landscapes*. Unpublished manuscript, copy in Herefordshire SMR

McOmish, D., Field, D. and Brown, G. 2002. *The Field Archaeology of the Salisbury Plain training Area.* English Heritage. London

Macklin, M. G. and Lewin, J. 2003. River sediments, great floods and centennial-scale climate change. *Journal of Quaternary Science*, **18(2)**, 101-105

Morris, E. L. 1982, Iron Age pottery from western Britain: another petrological study, in I. Freestone, C. Johns and T. Potter (eds.) *Current research in ceramics: thin section studies*, Brit. Mus. Occas. Pap. **32**, 15-25

Morris, E L 1983, *Salt and ceramic exchange in western Britain during the first millenium BC*, unpubl PhD thesis, Univ Southampton.

Morris, E L, 1992, Petrology of the prehistoric pottery in S Woodiwiss (ed), 1992 *Iron Age and Roman Salt Production and the Medieval Town of Droitwich. Excavations at the Old Bowling Green and Friar Street*, CBA Res Rep **81**, fiche 3, B6-B9

Muir, R. 2000. *The New Reading the Landscape.* University of Exeter Press. Exeter

Needham, S. 1990. Middle Bronze Age Ceremonial Weapons: new finds from Oxborough, Norfolk and Essex/Kent. Antiquaries Journal vol 70, 239-252

Needham, S. 1996. Chronology and Periodisation in the British Bronze Age. Randsborg, K. (ed) *Absolute Chronology: Archaeological Europe 2500-500BC, Acta Archaeologica* 67. *Acta Archaeologica Supplementa Vol I,* 121-40

Needham, S, C Bronk Ramsay, D Coombs, C Cartwright, P Pettit. 1997. An Independent Chronology for British Bronze Age Metalwork: the results of the Oxford Radiocarbon Accelerator Programme. Archaeological Journal vol **154**, 55-107

Oxford Archaeology. 2002. *Management of Archaeological Sites in Arable Landscapes.* Report prepared for DEFRA. Oxford

Peacock, D. P. S. 1967, 'Romano-British Pottery Production in the Malvern District of Worcestershire.' *Trans. Worcestershire Archaeol. Soc.,* 3rd Ser. **1** (1965-7), 15-28

Peacock, D P S, 1968, 'A Petrological Study of Certain Iron Age Pottery from Western England.' *Proc Prehist Soc,* **13**, 414-427

Pryor, F. 2001. The Flag Fen Basin. Archaeology and environment of a Fenland landscape. English Heritage, Swindon

Rackham, O. 1986. *The History of the Countryside.* Phoenix Giant. London

Pye, W. R. 1970. Mills on the River Arrow inHaliwell, P. R. (ed.) 1970, Herefordshire Archaeological News **18**

Rawes, B, 1982, Gloucester Severn Valley Ware: a study of the Roman pottery forms, *Trans Bristol Gloucester Archaeol Soc*, **100**, 33-46

Ray, K. 2001. *Medieval Towns in Herefordshire: a Management Review.* Herefordshire Archaeology Report **20**. Hereford

Ray, K. and White, P. 2004. *Herefordshire's Historic Landscape: A Characterisation.* Herefordshire Studies in Archaeology Series, Vol **1**. Herefordshire Archaeology. Hereford

RCHME. 1934. *An Inventory of the Historical Monuments in Herefordshire, Vol. 3 – North West.* HMSO. London

Renfrew, C. 2003a. *Grove Farm, Pembridge: A Whole Farm Archaeological Survey.* Herefordshire Archaeology Report **104**. Hereford

Renfrew, C. 2003b. *Titley Court: A Whole Farm Archaeological Survey.* Herefordshire Archaeology Report **108**. Hereford

Renfrew, C. 2003c. *Broadward Hall, Leominster: A Whole Farm Archaeological Survey.* Herefordshire Archaeology Report **109**. Hereford

Renfrew, C. 2003d. *Newburn Farm, Kington: A Whole Farm Archaeological Survey.* Herefordshire Archaeology Report **110**. Hereford

Renfrew, C. 2003e. *Lowe farm, Pembridge: A Whole Farm Archaeological Survey.* Herefordshire Archaeology Report **111**. Hereford

Renfrew, C. 2003f. *Court House Farm, Eardisland: A Whole Farm Archaeological Survey.* Herefordshire Archaeology Report **112**. Hereford

Renfrew, C. 2003g *Folly Farm, Eardisland: A Whole Farm Archaeological Survey.* Herefordshire Archaeology Report **115**. Hereford

Richardson, A. 2003, *An analysis of the pottery from the 2002 excavations at Moorcroft Farm and Cold Furrow, Lyonshall*, Unpublished BA Dissertation, The University of Cardiff

Rimmington, N. 2000. Proactive Earthwork Management on Hadrian's Wall World Heritage Site, in: McGlade, D. (ed.) *Erosion Control on Archaeological Earthworks and Recreational Paths.* Northumberland County Council. Northumberland, 15- 18

Seager Smith, R., and Davies, S. M. 1993, Black Burnished Ware Type Series. The Roman Pottery from Excavations at Greyhound Yard, Dorchester, Dorset. Wessex Archaeology. (Off printed from P. J. Woodward, S. M. Davies, and A. H. Graham, 'Excavations at the Old Methodist Chapel and Greyhound Yard, Dorchester 1981-1984,' *Dorset Natur. Hist. Archaeol. Soc. Monogr. Ser.* **12**)

Selfe, P. 2002. *Eardisland Archaeology.* Bulletin produced by Eardisland Oral History Group

Stanford, S. C. 1974, *Croft Ambrey. Excavations carried out for the Woolhope Naturalists' Field Club (Herefordshire) 1960-1966*

Stanford, S. C. 1991. *The Archaeology of the Welsh Marches.* Private Publication. Hereford

Thorby, T. (ed) 2000. *Staunton's Millennium Book.* Trustees of the Staunton-on-Arrow Village Hall

Tomber, R. S.1985, Pottery, in A. R. Wilmot and S. P. Q. Rahtz, 99-145, Fiche frames 1-59

Tomber, R. and Dore, J. 1998, *The National Roman Fabric Reference Collection. A handbook.* MoLAS Monogr. **2**

Trump, B. 1962. The Origin and Development of British Middle Bronze Age Rapiers. Proceedings of the Prehistoric Society vol 28, 80-102

Webster, P. V. 1976, Severn Valley Ware: A Preliminary Study. *Trans. Bristol Gloucestershire Archaeol. Soc.* **94**, 18-46.

Webster, P. 1996, *Roman Samian Pottery in Britain.* CBA Practical Handbook in Archaeology **13**.

White, P. 2001. *The Impact of Potato Cultivation on Archaeological Sites in Herefordshire. A Preliminary Study.* Herefordshire Archaeology Report **44**. Hereford

White, P. 2003a. *Admarsh Coppice, Eardisland: A Site Investigation.* Herefordshire Archaeology Report **94**. Hereford

White, P. 2003b. *Upper Headlands, The Grove, Staunton-on-Arrow: A Site Investigation.* Herefordshire Archaeology Report **95**. Hereford

White, P. 2003c. *Top Hales, The Leen, Pembridge: A Site Investigation.* Herefordshire Archaeology Report **102**. Hereford

White, P. 2003d. *The Leen, Pembridge: A Whole Farm Archaeological Survey.* Herefordshire Archaeology Report **103**. Hereford

White, P. 2003e. *Woodbrook Farm, Kington: A Whole Farm Archaeological Survey.* Herefordshire Archaeology Report **105**. Hereford

White, P. 2003f. *Luntley Court Farm, Pembridge: A Whole Farm Archaeological Survey.* Herefordshire Archaeology Report **106**. Hereford

White, P. 2003g. *Arrow Mill, Eardisland: A Whole Farm Archaeological Survey.* Herefordshire Archaeology Report **107**. Hereford

White, P. 2003h. *Little Broome, Eardisland: A Whole Farm Archaeological Survey.* Herefordshire Archaeology Report **113**. Hereford

White, P. 2003i. *Broom Farm, Eardisland: A Whole Farm Archaeological Survey.* Herefordshire Archaeology Report **114**. Hereford

White, P. and Renfrew C. 2003a. *Ox Pasture and Middle Field, The Leen, Pembridge: Site Investigation.* Herefordshire Archaeology Report **96**. Hereford

White, P and Renfrew, C. 2003b. *Court of Noke, Pembridge: A Whole Farm Archaeological Survey.* Herefordshire Archaeology Report **116**. Hereford
Whitehead, D. 2001. *A Survey of Historic Parks and Gardens of Herefordshire.* Hereford and Worcester Gardens Trust

Williams, D. F. 1977, The Romano-British Black-burnished Industry: An Essay on Characterization by Heavy Mineral Analysis. In D. P. S. Peacock (ed.) 1977, *Pottery and early commerce: characterization and trade in Roman and later ceramics*, 163-220.

Williams, D. 2003. *Wapley Hill, Staunton-on-Arrow: Woodland Survey.* Herefordshire Archaeology Report **83**. Hereford

Williamson, T. 1987. Early Co-axial Field Systems on the East Anglian Boulder Clays. *Proceedings of the Prehistoric Society*, **53**, 419-431

Willis, S. forthcoming, The Iron Age and Roman pottery, in R. Jackson, *The Roman Settlement of Ariconium, near Weston-under-Penyard, Herefordshire: An assessment and synthesis of the evidence.*

Wilmot, A. R. and Rahtz, S. P. Q. 1985, An Iron Age and Roman settlement outside Kenchester (Magnis), Herefordshire. Excavations 1977-79, *Transactions of the Woolhope Naturalists' Field Club*, **45**, 36-185.

Woodiwiss, S. 1989. Salvage Excavation of a Beaker Burial from Aymestrey. *Transactions of the Woolhope Naturalists Field Club*, 46 (II), 169-76.

Zaluckyj, S. 2001. *Mercia . The Anglo-Saxon Kingdom of Central England.* Logaston Press. Herefordshire